RACE TO AMAZING

•••

YOUR FAST TRACK
TO SALES LEADERSHIP

•••

KRISTA S. MOORE

ISBN: 978-1-7324694-0-2

Published by K.Coaching Inc.
https://kcoaching.com

K.COACHING,INC
ignite your potential

In memory of my father, Dick Shaffer, and his mother, Grandma Betty

CONTENTS

INTRODUCTION

"Twenty years from now you'll be more disappointed by the things
you didn't do than by the ones that you did do, so throw off the bowlines,
sail away from safe harbors, catch the trade winds in your sails.
Explore. Dream. Discover."

—Mark Twain

I once heard that when we think we have it all figured out, when we think we know all we need to know about our product, industry, business, area of expertise, or leadership, that's when we regress. That's when we grow stagnant, lose focus, and become bored, complacent, and unproductive. You may have heard the analogy that people are like trees: you're either growing or you're dying. *Race to Amazing* is about that growth, about the personal developmental path you choose to be on, whereby you continue to learn, develop, and grow, striving to be the best you can be. In this book I invite you to prepare for that race, to be driven to completion, and to enjoy the positive impact on yourself and others. I'm excited for you to experience the journey of self-discovery and intentional leadership development.

As a sales leader for twenty-five years, I've learned that it's much easier to reach the pinnacle of success with the help of others, and that there's no need to go it alone. I believe that when you voluntarily seek a coach or a mentor or join a mastermind group, you're ready to get started on the Race to Amazing. As the founder of K.Coaching, Inc. and an executive and business coach, I have the wonderful job of helping already successful leaders ignite their full potential and win their personal race. I'm passionate about what I do every day and relish the thought of helping others achieve greatness and reach their personal and professional goals. I want to do the same for you—to be your coach and guide as you begin your journey with this book.

The race doesn't have a time clock or necessarily a clear path or a trophy at the end, but it does have a purpose: to win that amazing leader status and the accomplishments that come along with it. Sometimes the race might be against another person for a title or position, but most often the race is with the voice in your head that tells you "It can't be done," or "You're not good enough," or puts fear and doubt into your spirit that will stop you in your tracks.

My coaching approach and the Race to Amazing program begins with you clarifying your vision of what success looks like and then identifying the barriers that are getting in your way. The result is creating coaching objectives and a developmental path that will reveal your amazing, authentic self.

It begins with self-discovery through personal reflection and an open and honest relationship with yourself, where you can feel vulnerable yet safe. You must also begin with the end in mind, for this is your personal race to discover who you are and who you want to be. Then, you must accept the challenge and realize that it's a journey that will take time and commitment. Ultimately, you need the passion and desire to *win*. Winning as defined by *you*, that gives you the awesome sense of accomplishment and the incredible feeling of "I did it! I made it! I have arrived!" It is also for the personal reward of seeing others flourish and become successful under your guidance and experiencing the positive impact you can have on many people's lives. Ultimately, at the end of your race you're living each day with purpose, with passion, and being the amazing leader you're meant to be.

Regardless of your current situation, circumstance, or frame of reference on this subject, I ask you to begin and end this journey— *your* journey—with me. Allow me to be your personal coach. There will be times when we disagree, or when you believe you don't need my help, or when you've encountered an area well understood and executed. I ask you to not stop the race, take a detour, or apply self-imposed shortcuts. There will be times when you feel that you've already won the race, after you've completed a task or finished a project or checked another item off your to-do list. Other times you might feel like you're in a rat race, roaming endlessly in a state of confusion and uncertainty. But when you feel exhausted and ready to throw in the towel, don't give up on your dreams in search of an easier way or a different path. When you're feeling uncomfortable or overwhelmed, it's likely fear in disguise and it's getting the best of you. The race may slow down, or pause at times, but remember, it's a purposeful journey, so always have the end in mind. Don't give up, and know that I'm your coach, running beside you, cheering you on along the way.

This journey is about business and leadership development, but I don't believe that there's anyone reading this book who hasn't thought about their purpose in life and wondered if they're living the life that's intended for them. Perhaps you're wondering right now, with uncertainty, yet with an insatiable yearning to understand and wanting for more out of life, love, and relationships? Maybe you want to finally have work-life balance, clearer goals, more meaningful relationships, or to be liked or respected at all costs? For most people, the race is simply striving to be the best you can be, to gain clarity on what you need to do differently or better to be more fulfilled, while discovering and being who you were always meant to be.

With *Race to Amazing*, not only can *you* get there, but you can bring your family, friends, and coworkers along with you. Our intentions, behaviors, attitudes, and actions influence those around us in a positive or negative way. You may want to announce your intentions to begin this race and solicit supporters. More importantly, know that you're not on this journey alone. You're not the only one seeking answers and the support of others who care about you and your happiness.

As an executive coach who's worked with thousands of business owners, sales leaders, mid-level managers, and sales professionals, I've discovered many common themes and roadblocks. In *Race to Amazing*, I'll share with you the key findings, challenges, proven methods, and best practices from many of our clients. In addition, I'll share my journey and lessons learned, along with some connection exercises to help you get to your endgame faster.

This isn't a typical self-help book, or a business and leadership strategy manual. Consider it your personal guide to leadership self-discovery, one that will help you implement practical business strategies and create an effective and rewarding leadership style. As you go through *Race to Amazing* and break through the finish line, you'll not only have a sense of accomplishment, but the proven results that you're looking for in your business. No race happens without action and no race will be successful without preparation. This book will help you do both. Remember, *Race to Amazing* is about your journey to be your best self, so you can feel and do amazing things.

This is your journey—not mine. It's what you make of it. I'm here to be your coach, to help you gain clarity of vision and purpose, to cheer you on and guide you back on course. This is all for the purpose and sincere desire to help you become the amazing leader, manager, or person you're meant to be.

This book is my way of giving back to everyone who helped me along the way, to honor my God-given talents, and to live my life with the same purpose and passion I desire for others. I'm certain my "spiritual space" is business, and I believe there's much more I can do to help others by sharing my experiences, doing what I love, and letting that childhood dream come out. This book is my way of serving the masses in a bigger way, by helping individuals who are curious and beginning to make shifts, by helping companies or teams embrace best practices and implement change, or helping emerging leaders accept their challenge.

It's time for *you* to lead by example, and impact the lives of others.

CHAPTER 1—WINNING WITH CHANGE

"Don't wish it were easier, wish you were better."

—Jim Rohn

As an eager and restless child growing up in a small coal-mining town in Western Pennsylvania, I didn't have much exposure to the world of sales. Most of the men in the neighborhood worked in the coal mines or steel mills, and my family members worked at my grandfather's strip mining company. Everyone, that is, except my father. He was considered the black sheep of the family because he wanted to build something of his own. He enjoyed working with his hands and wasn't afraid to get them dirty. In my younger days, I remember him constantly working odd jobs at unusual hours to provide for our family. He installed three-hundred-foot electric power lines across Western Pennsylvania and Ohio, started his own asphalt paving company, and drove a snowplow for the state of Pennsylvania during the cold winter months. I remember him saying that when it snowed it was "pennies from heaven" because he was able to go to work.

As I look back on those years, we didn't have a lot of money, but there was nothing that I needed or wanted that wasn't provided for me. I'm sure that any savings our family had was spent on the occasional beach vacation to the Blue Star Motel at the Jersey Shore. And there were always plenty of Christmas gifts for me and my three brothers, and we could count on new outfits and shoes for church on Easter Sunday.

I distinctly remember the day that things changed for our family. My father told me that he was changing his job and he was going to be a salesman. I was eight years old at the time, and I remember laughing and saying to him, "Daddy, you're not a salesman. Why do you want to be a salesman?"

A family friend got him involved in a company called Bestline, which in those days was equivalent to Amway, and somewhat of a pyramid scheme. He was going to have a career selling detergent, disinfectant, and home cleaning products. He worked hard to get as many friends and family members selling Bestline as he could.

I recall helping him carry cases of carpet cleaner, air freshener, laundry detergent, and shampoo to the cellar of our small home. He and my mom flew to Florida for their first sales conference and convention. That experience was life-altering; it changed the course of his life and mine.

My father came back from that trip with renewed energy and the confidence to take on the world. He had heard the legendary Jim Rohn speak at the conference and purchased his motivational cassette tapes. All of a sudden, he was blaring motivational cassettes throughout the house. I remember hearing Rohn's prominent voice, loud and clear, over and over again as those tapes played seemingly day in and day out. Rohn would often refer to change saying, "For things to change, you've got to change. When you change, everything will change for you. When you get better, everything will get better for you." I remember hearing profound messages like, "You don't have to change your market, your plans, the economy, countries, or circumstances, but rather look within and see if you can change yourself for the better."

At the impressionable age of eight, those words had significant impact on how I viewed the world, how I would deal with challenging circumstances, and ultimately who I am today. At that time, I saw my father changing. He was not only learning a new trade, but becoming a businessman who was thinking more strategically, developing selling skills, and demonstrating leadership. He was the consummate salesman and truly became a sales leader for his company.

Fast-forward forty-four years; it's ironic how Jim Rohn's messages and my father's mentorship and spirit still influence me. They've inspired and guided me in my twenty-year career as a sales leader and today they're even more meaningful to me, as an entrepreneur and executive coach. Remember, if you want things to change, *you* need to change. Race to Amazing is about awareness and making intentional changes for the better.

Developing selling skills and being an effective sales manager isn't something you can learn overnight. Too often sales reps are hired straight out of college, put into a role that they may be unprepared for, and given some sales training. They typically struggle to succeed. Sales managers are assigned to manage people and processes because they've had a successful career as a sales representative. Two different skill sets are required for success, but still, top sales reps are frequently slated for the sales management role.

In my experience, sales leadership can be the most crucial position within any organization, yet more often than not the individual at the helm isn't fully equipped or trained. They seldom realize the impact of their leadership style on others and the ultimate success of the company. For me, as a business coach focused on sales and leadership development, I've learned this firsthand and witness it daily.

Whether you're a business owner or a sales manager, there's no need to go one more day without being an effective sales leader. Your daily interactions, as well as how you lead, communicate, motivate, and inspire, can have a tremendous impact on those that follow you. With Race to Amazing, you'll learn a proven model for sales leadership development and the tried-and-true steps to becoming an amazing leader. The race is intended to be fast-paced, with hurdles along the way. But you'll learn a step-by-step system that can make the difference between winning and losing. It can make the difference between success and failure. But first you need to begin.

So, are you ready?

Do You Want to Change?

Like most things worth having, this process will require some work. In the words of Jim Rohn, "If you want things to be better, then you need to be better." What do you need to change, or do better or different, to be more successful and achieve a specific goal, success, or level of happiness? This personal discovery to understand what you need to change can be daunting. There's no prescription, cookie-cutter resolution, or magic wand you can wave. Everyone is unique in their desires and circumstances, but the methodology to "get there" and arrive at that "better place" tends to be the same.

As a leadership coach, I see various levels of readiness from clients when it comes to making the decision to pursue leadership development and taking the necessary actions. Review the following three examples to help determine your readiness for your Race to Amazing.

Top Level: The Coach

When you proactively seek a mentor or a coach or join a mastermind group, you've taken the first step in getting ready for development and preparing for change. You enter a coaching engagement, understand what coaching is all about, have a high level of commitment to the program, and possess a great deal of self-awareness. Mentally, and often physically healthy, you're prepared to be vulnerable, and are ready to identify the missing piece that will unlock a world of possibilities. At this level of readiness, you realize that what you need to tweak or change will affect not only yourself, but the lives of many. This one small shift in how you behave, react, or communicate can have a significant impact on the success of your teams, spouse, family, and community.

At this level, you're highly intuitive. You're all in, and you understand the analogy and the importance of going from 211 degrees to 212 degrees—just one degree of change. At 212 degrees, great things happen. It's the boiling point, where water turns to steam, which now can power engines and move trains! With a coach approach to leadership, you will realize what a small shift in behavior can do for others and your own success. So often I've seen how one insight or applied new skill such as improved listening or empathy can make a remarkable difference in how others respond to your sales leadership style.

Coach Joe

 Joe is a highly accomplished leader in his field, yet he is continuously looking for ways to advance his career, build followers, and create future leaders for his company. Since Joe is acutely aware and results-oriented, he sees a direct correlation between his leadership style and the measurable performance of others. Joe has high core values of trust, respect, and principle. He is responsible for $180 million in revenue, generated by thirteen sales executives throughout North America. He manages them through regular team conference calls, and travels into various territories to work with the sales executives as often as he can.

Through coaching conversations, we discovered that Joe was struggling to effectively lead and manage his direct reports. Joe began to realize that he was using remote management as his built-in excuse for not giving his sales executives the time and support they needed. He found himself rationalizing rather than prioritizing. Through coaching, Joe decided to make one-on-one conversations with his team a priority. He committed to making proactive, outbound, personal phone calls to each of them every week and a half. The agenda for that call was simple:

give them some of his focused time. Joe scheduled it on his calendar, made it a priority, and is now seeing amazing results. The low performers now see him as more approachable and reach out to him more often for guidance and direction, resulting in a 6 percent increase in sales revenue. The high performers appreciate the attention and are motivated by him showing that he cares and knows where they stand. Joe identified one small area that was lacking, took action, and as a result is getting the desired effect. The key was that Joe was ready and willing to learn and apply even the simplest change to see if he could get better results.

Mid-Level: Nice Guy

These individuals are often referred to as the "nice guys" and are typically seen more as a friend than a boss or leader. If you're at or near mid-level, you may enter into a coaching or mentorship relationship because you know that you need to change how you manage people, but are skeptical or reluctant to try anything new and different.

Leaders at this level may not like holding others accountable and are uncomfortable giving constructive feedback or presenting consequences to underperformers. They tend to be well-liked, successful in building relationships, and have the loyalty of their employees. However, at the end of the day, they're moderately successful and seemingly complacent.

This can be a business owner who thinks their only challenge is time management, or a corporate sales leader who is assigned a coach to help them with their development. Regardless, they enter the coaching relationship apprehensive and reluctant, wearing blinders that are difficult to remove.

Mid-level leaders usually have good intentions and appear willing to make adjustments, but the execution of new ideas and changes may weigh heavy on their hearts, causing them to look for excuses. This makes it difficult to make the necessary changes and leads to behavior such as avoiding uncomfortable conversations or taking longer to address challenging situations. The result is no action, which stalls their Race to Amazing.

Tom: Everyone's Friend

 Tom runs a small, independent, business supplies company, generating $4 million in revenue with three outside business-to-business sales representatives. Over the years, he has enjoyed year-over-year sales growth with limited day-to-day sales management. With the downturn in the economy and the competition becoming more aggressive, Tom was losing business and his sales reps weren't bringing in new accounts fast enough to make up the difference. Tom contacted our company to receive coaching and consulting on ways he could motivate his salespeople to sell more. We quickly discovered that the sales reps didn't have quotas, activity goals, or consequences for poor performance. Through coaching conversations, Tom realized that this lack of accountability was the business culture that he created and the reason his sales reps had become complacent. Tom wasn't interested in letting go of people who had contributed to the success of his business over the years.

Since Tom was emotionally connected to them, both personally and professionally, getting him to change his "nice guy" style would be extremely difficult. Tom needed to discover one or two things he could change that would have the greatest impact on the growth of his business as well as his ability to manage others more effectively.

During one of our coaching conversations, Tom committed to having a conversation with each sales rep to address one area that he would like them to improve on, and to informing them that he would be monitoring their progress. We wanted to make it rather simple, something that he could do well while building his confidence in his new approach. We created a conversation guide for Tom to use to ask questions rather than tell others what to do. By asking questions, Tom was successful in getting the sales reps to talk about their thoughts and feelings towards business being down, while getting them to commit to a goal of more proactive sales calls. The sales reps also committed to reporting their progress back to Tom during weekly team meetings. Two out of the three sales representatives responded favorably by more than doubling their appointments. This was certainly a step in the right direction.

At this mid-level of leadership, you still can make shifts that change behaviors. It just might be at a slower pace.

Low-Level: Missing in Action (MIA)

Low-level managers can be the most hard-headed of all. It's unlikely that they're even reading this book. But if you identify with this level, you're already a successful leader in your own right, or your own mind. However, you may not be fully aware of the impact, positive and negative, that your current style has on others. You may be in your comfort zone, feeling satisfied with yourself and your success. This often is the result of not being challenged or held accountable by a manager or director. Even worse, your ego may get in the way of progress and you may believe that you're invincible or untouchable.

MIA leaders are just that: missing in action. This is about mentally being absent, rather than not showing up for work. The low-level MIA managers are unaware of their shortcomings, and believe they're at their best. They're reluctant to change who they are for anyone. This is seen in both large and small businesses, where there hasn't been a focus on leadership development and where a traditional autocratic management style has been the norm.

Many successful businesses have low-level leaders, and getting them to realize their potential or putting them on a fast track to amazing leadership might seem impossible. Imagine the future of those companies that are ready and willing to develop their MIA leaders. They would be identifying high-potential employees, investing in the next generation, retaining the right people, and leading by example. Often the MIA leader may not know what they don't know, or hasn't had exposure to amazing leadership. That's where coaching really works.

The coach helps create awareness around the possibilities, while understanding and agreeing on what needs to change or improve. The coach supports them through their actions until the necessary changes become habit. At that point, the possibilities are endless, and they begin to feel and see the difference that they make in their business success and in the lives of those who work for them.

In my experience, the main difference between companies that are hitting the ball out of the park and those that are complacent and slow to grow is effective sales leadership. Statistics show that

78 percent of employees leave their job because of their manager. What if more MIA's could get into the race?

MIA: That Was Me

 Early on in my career, I was a low-level manager. I was that person who was not aware and didn't realize the impact of my leadership style and actions. I had no idea that my team could actually achieve more if I was a better leader. In 1982, I began my career in customer service, as the eighth employee of a small computer supplies company in St. Louis, Missouri. I quickly moved into an inside telemarketing sales position, which we called "dialing for dollars," making calls to federal government offices throughout the United States, basically selling them anything they wanted to buy. After three years of telemarketing sales, I moved to a new sales office in Northern Virginia, calling on larger federal agencies like the FBI, CIA, and the Pentagon.

It was a fun time, until they asked me to be the sales manager, just because I was pretty good at sales. At the time, it seemed like a natural career progression, but I quickly realized that I had no experience or knowledge about how to manage people and lead a sales organization. I remember asking my boss, who was in St. Louis at the time, for help or training and he told me to "Just show them the ropes. Take the reps out in the field, and show them how it's done." I later learned this is called a "Pied Piper Management Style," whereby you gain followers by having people watch and emulate your style. This is typically not effective long-term, because they're not learning from their mistakes and the Pied Piper manager is telling or directing, rather than providing feedback and coaching. But at that time, it seemed to work. We built a successful team and grew it to a $12 million location within six years, while having a blast along the way. I was thinking, "I got this!" I'll be the first to admit that our success was based on luck, hiring some great people, relentless focus, and a competitive sales spirit, not effective sales leadership. I was young and inexperienced as a manager and leader, and was oblivious to the possibilities of how I could influence others through strategic vision and coaching.

Then in 1993, I was asked to move to Chicago to lead the startup of another new location for the company. At the time I had a two-year-old, a two-month-old, and a husband with no job. There I was, day one with no employees and no clients. I still had no formal management training or leadership development, so I quickly resorted to doing what I knew best and had worked for me in the past: selling myself and teaching new hires the ropes. We had great success, selling $4 million in our first year, which gained the attention of Boise Cascade Office Products, who eventually acquired the company.

Beginning to work for a larger organization with a management system, sales processes, and rules was certainly an adjustment. This is when I realized I was a low-level MIA. I vividly remember the first day I met my new boss. I was telling him about myself, my outstanding career progression, and my sales success. He stopped me from nervously bragging and said, "I don't care who you are, or what you've done. All I care about is what you're going to do for Boise Cascade Office Products." I realized that day that I was acquired, not hired, and that I had a lot to learn.

Shortly after that, I was told that I needed to go to management school. (Remember, I'm a low-level MIA, with no self-awareness or readiness to develop.) I heard my boss refer to me as a "raw manager." I thought, "What am I, a piece of meat?" Basically, I didn't know what I didn't know, but I was appalled. I remember saying, "Management school? Why do I need to go to management school? Look at my track record on building successful teams and hitting sales quotas."

Begrudgingly, I attended a formal management course at their corporate headquarters. It took me a few hours to get engaged, because I kept thinking I shouldn't be there and what I could be doing that would be more productive than sitting there listening to the instructor. I remember hearing the instructor say, "People want recognition and to know that you care." I muttered to myself, "Their recognition is in their commission check."

After a while, I started to truly listen to what was being said. I enjoyed the success stories of how others applied some of the techniques and saw terrific results with their employees. The successful teams were clear on the mission and vision of the company. They understood their goals and expectations, and were inspired and motivated for achievement.

Later that afternoon, on a break, I decided to test one of the theories I learned on one of my new sales reps, Mike. He was doing a great job. We had spent a lot of time together in the field, closing deals and high fiving. I went downstairs where my team was working, walked up to Mike, put my hand on his shoulder (it was legal to do that in those days), looked at him straight in the eyes, and said, "I know you've only worked here for a short period of time, but I want you to know I think you're doing a terrific job. If you keep it up, you'll have a very successful career within our company." He looked at me, bewildered, with a slight smirk on his face, and said, "What? Did you learn that up in management class?"

That was the exact moment I realized how transparent I was. I knew that I needed to improve who I was as a leader. My own team and my boss helped me to see that despite my previous success, I was a raw manager and there was a lot for me to learn in order to become an effective leader. I learned that the perceptions of others mattered. I began to realize that how well we listen, understand, and communicate can greatly influence the actions, moods, and behaviors of others, ultimately impacting the success or failure of individuals and companies.

I learned that I could truly influence behavior in a positive way by understanding others and what motivates them. I also understood that other people's core values were not necessarily the same as mine, and that it was OK. What motivated them every day could be very different from what inspired me, or the person sitting next to them. Most importantly, I realized that my job as a sales manager and leader was more than just showing those who worked for me how to do their job. I had a lot to learn to up my game.

It was when I experienced this self-awareness at management school that I took leadership development to heart and began focusing on self-improvement. I must admit, I went a little crazy: I began enrolling in leadership development courses, and read every article and book on management and motivation I could get my hands on. My car was full of home-study courses on cassette by Zig Ziglar, Dale Carnegie, and my obvious first choice and daily favorite, Jim Rohn. His words, "If you want things to change, then you need to change" resonated with me and took on a whole new meaning.

I began intentionally practicing new skills, changing how I approached people and situations, while simultaneously watching the impact and measuring the results. I was personally changing and, as a result, things were changing for the better around me. It was a transformation that took time, but was instantly obvious to those who worked with me, to my family, and to my employer.

All of a sudden, our team saw traction and momentum like we had never seen before. We were winning big deals and exceeded our quota by double digits. We even closed a $1 million single order—the largest in the company's history. Over the next five years, I was more strategic in my approach to business and more structured in my management system. I began coaching others to be the best that they could be, rather than just telling them what to do. Ultimately, I was helping them build some of the most successful sales teams in the country.

CHAPTER 2—READY, SET...

"Always remember, your focus determines your reality."

—George Lucas

Before you begin your Race to Amazing you first must be aware and ready to focus on yourself. Do you know what you want to accomplish? Are you willing to get started? Are you passionate about the end results? Getting ready is easier said than done.

Yes, this race is a competition, but not necessarily a competition between you and someone else. It's a competition with the little voice in your head that's telling you that you can't change, feeding you lots of excuses or blame, and stalling your start.

Remember, the most successful leaders want to learn how to be more effective, be the best that they can be, truly affect change, execute ideas, and implement their vision. They want to build followers, a network, or a community, and earn the respect of many, while meeting goals and achieving financial results. More importantly, successful leaders want to have a positive impact on the lives of others, which often becomes their purpose and their passion. When you can clearly see what your endgame looks like, you'll be ready to start. But know there's no need to go it alone. With *Race to Amazing*, I'm here as your coach to guide and cheer you along the way. In addition, you have many friends, family, and coworkers who care about you and want to see you succeed.

Prep Activities

The activities in this chapter will help in your readiness and preparation. These exercises are often used at the beginning of a client coaching engagement to create the right mindset, before you begin your journey. Whether you're a coach, a nice guy, or MIA, everyone should start at the beginning with a clean windshield and a view of the end in mind.

· ·

Prep Activity #1: Chuck Your Junk

Write on a piece of paper all of the negative thoughts that tend to fill your head, the thoughts that often hold you back from progress. This is the junk that floats in and out of your mind on a daily or weekly basis. It could be negative memories, thoughts of people who irritate you, or experiences that create self-doubt or tarnish your confidence.

After you spend a fair amount of time with your junk, read what you wrote once again, then crumple it up and throw it out. The mental exercise of thinking through these negative thoughts, then the physical act of crumpling them up and throwing them in the garbage is a great way to create the mindset you need to start your race and begin the process—without fear, uncertainty, or doubt.

· ·

Prep Activity #2: Write Letters

 This exercise is similar to the Chuck Your Junk exercise, but on a deeper, more focused level. Write a letter to someone who you have something to say to, but never said. Perhaps they did something to you that was unethical, dishonest, or deceitful. They may have hurt you emotionally and you've never been able to shake it; the feeling is like an old wound that won't heal. You could write to an old friend, with whom your relationship has ended. You may miss them, have never spoken about it, and still don't understand what happened. Or you could write to a family member who has caused you great pain or strife and you have strong words for them, but know it's best not to express your feelings in a verbal altercation. It could be to a former boss or employer, with whom you had a falling out and never got to have your final word. The list goes on, but you get it, right?

I remember when I first learned about this exercise during

my business coaching certification program and did it myself. I doubted the effects of the concept and was uninterested in taking the time to write letters, but I needed to as part of a homework assignment. Reluctantly, I ventured to the backyard on a beautiful spring day to lie in a lawn chair with a glass of sweet tea, and let my thoughts and feelings flow as I composed three letters. I'm proud to report that it was an absolutely amazing feeling and I highly recommend this exercise to all of my clients.

My first letter was to the CEO of the company that I resigned from, letting him know how unimpressed I was with his leadership and that he was the main reason I didn't accept the offer to stay on with the company. Another letter went to a previous boss who I felt had an anger management issue and needed to control his emotions in the workplace. I told him that no one deserved to be treated with such disrespect.

Now, the best part is, you can mail the letters or choose not to. I chose not to. For me, the process of getting those deep-seated thoughts and feelings out on paper was all I needed. I also took one step further: I forgave them. Forgiveness is a wonderful and powerful act. It lightened my heart, cleared my mind, and mended my soul. I was now ready for coaching.

• •

Prep Activity #3: Thinking Time

 Although I recommend all of these activities, this one is non-negotiable. If you're going to begin your Race to Amazing, you need to get some thinking time on your calendar. This is your personal time, when you physically and mentally remove yourself from the hustle and bustle of your workday, and life in general. Too often, our day-to-day responsibilities can be all-consuming as we are taking care of others, at work and at home, and we often forget to take care of ourselves. I suggest scheduling time for yourself, just like you might for an appointment. Then, make it sacred, so no one can take it from you. For some of you, this might be in a coffee shop, on the treadmill, or sitting in a special, quiet spot at home or in your office. It might become part of the time you set aside for daily meditation or prayer. You may discover the ideal time to schedule it is before or after the time you're spending reading this book. This will keep you on track, as you'll be practicing the concepts and applying them to your life and current circumstances. The important thing is that you do it, and that you dedicate life's most precious resource, time, for you! Not only is this a best practice for successful leaders, it can become a wonderful habit that will provide you peace of mind, reflection, and relaxation for years to come.

• •

Prep Activity #4: Self-Reflection

Often in business coaching, as in life, people show up with their best foot forward and their happy face on. It's natural to portray yourself as the person that you want others to see. This is your public persona. But who are you at your core? What kind of leader do you really want to be? Even though you may exude a strong desire and confidence to accomplish a great deal, you need to trust your instincts, get quiet, and be vulnerable to reveal your true self. Would you ever enter a physical race without being conditioned or mentally prepared to win, or at least finish? This is why I'm certain that self-reflection and discovery are necessary to have a successful race.

Many successful people have mastered the skills of introspection and self-awareness. They're able to naturally influence others in a positive way and are always willing and able to learn more. Then there are some who have a lower level of awareness or who haven't taken the time to dive deeply into understanding themselves or others' motivations. This makes it difficult to rationalize the impact their leadership style can have on other people's actions and business success. They're just not able to connect those dots and, in some cases, could be considered "not coachable." That's why awareness, readiness, and preparation are so important—from a coach's perspective, these are required before we can work together on the areas that are holding you or your company back from progress. Self-reflection can take place during your thinking time, but we'll dive more deeply into awareness and self-reflection in Chapter 3.

Mirror, Mirror

 Soon after starting my coaching practice, I was hired by my first client, Dave, a small business owner, to work with his sales team. I was to assess what was holding them back from being successful, then recommend and facilitate some additional sales training. The first step was to do some discovery and analyze the company's strengths, weaknesses, opportunities, and threats (SWOT).

It was also a time for the team to get together as a group and determine some focus areas for the new year. When I arrived, the business owner was quick to say that he wouldn't be at the meeting because he was too busy.

Against my better judgment, I conducted the meeting without him present, but I also felt that the team might be more open and honest if he wasn't in the room. I would still be able to collect valid information, understand the current culture, dynamics, and circumstances to do my assessment, and offer recommendations.

As I walked through the SWOT analysis with the employees, it was clear that the company had a fair number of strengths and opportunities for growth. Then we got to the discussion of threats, which we defined as what was happening in their business, industry, or market that was serious, and what could be detrimental to the success of the organization but was out of their control. All of them were quick to say that *he*, the business owner, was the *threat*. They felt that he was out of touch with what was happening in the business. He wasn't in the office and therefore wasn't present enough to manage the day-to-day tasks. There was no question that there was a strong level of distrust between him and the employees. Keep in mind, I was trying to build a business on my own and this was one of my first clients. I really didn't want it to be going in this direction; after all, *he* was the one writing the check.

After we finished, I went into Dave's office and he asked me how it went. Before I could even respond, he said he thought it went well and wanted me to continue working with them on an ongoing basis. I was speechless. He wasn't even in the meeting and was clueless as to what the team thought of him and the negative impact he was having on his own company. I remember saying, "I'm sorry, I can't work with you, because I don't believe I can help you." He seemed very agitated and said, "What do you mean? What do you mean you can't help me?" I proceeded to tell him about the SWOT analysis and him being a big part of the problem. I also explained that if he wasn't interested in being involved and making some changes himself, then I wouldn't be able to help him or his business.

That meeting didn't end well, and I remember driving back to the airport thinking that I was totally crazy to turn down one of my first clients, but it just didn't feel right. It would have been a waste of his money and my time. He wasn't at all ready or aware of his leadership impact to begin any type of coaching relationship. He definitely lacked self-awareness.

There's a good ending to this story, although it took a few twists and turns. I received a phone call a few weeks later from Dave saying that he understood why I didn't accept the engagement and that he realized he needed to change in order for his business to improve. He also told me he was committed to coaching and asked if he could hire me as his executive coach. Today, he remains a very successful businessman, a close friend, and a client. He is proud of his achievements, and often reminds others that he was my first client, and then jokingly reveals that I fired him twice. All true. It may not always be a smooth course for your Race to Amazing, but it has to start with awareness and commitment.

• •

Prep Activity #5: Create a Lifeline

I first learned of this exercise when I joined the Entrepreneurs Organization (www.eonetwork.org), and was exposed to the EO Forums. This method was used for getting to know other forum members on a deeper level, as part of their small mastermind-type meeting format. Each member of the forum would have ten minutes to describe what the organization called their "lifeline" to the other members.

The essence of the lifeline is to plot your life along the age line indicating the significant events that represent the emotional highs and lows or best and worst memories. These events should date from the day you were born until the present. The end result should be a visual line graph, similar to the example below.

Lifeline Example

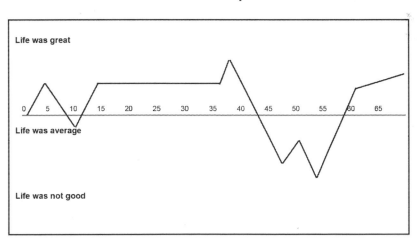

Your Lifeline

Life was great

```
  0    5    10   15   20   25   30   35   40   45   50   55   60   65
```

Life was average

Life was not good

Thoughtful reflection on the lifeline exercise can be an eye-opening experience, creating awareness that you're a collection of life experiences. With most coaching clients, using the lifeline exercise helps them identify significant events and circumstances that have contributed to their current habits and leadership style.

It's often your inherent core values and frame of reference that influence daily decision making. There are a number of triggers or influences that precipitate the changes we make in our lives; some happen abruptly, but most evolve over time. Your lifeline should also reveal that you control your life pace and direction through the choices and decisions you make.

· ·

Prep Activity #6: Lifeline Reflections

 Spend some time reviewing your lifeline and thinking through the following questions:

What common themes are represented in this lifeline exercise?

You can use what I discovered as examples for creating yours: Hard-working, Trust, Positive Attitude/Motivation, Mentorship, Speaking/Writing /Communications, Family/Faith in God, Team Building, Challenge/Adventure, Constant Learner, Creating/ Building/Startups

What types of experiences or events caused you to feel that life was great?

When your life was not so good, describe how you were feeling.

Which of your habits or behaviors today may have been created through your lifeline?

Are there any correlations between your lifeline experiences and your career choice?

What experiences had an impact on your leadership or management style?

Think back to when you were ten years old, approximately fourth or fifth grade. What memories come to mind? What were you doing when you were ten years old?

Your 10-Year-Old Self

At K.Coaching, we developed a process of discovering your life purpose, hidden talents, and dreams, by going back to your ten-year-old memories. Age ten has proven to be a significant age, before peer and social pressure have taken hold. There's evidence through our research that most people can begin to remember their childhood at, or close, to this age.

There's also research to show that at age ten is where purpose and passion meet, and when we are our most authentic selves.

We call this the Your 10-Year-Old Self process, and it's the subject of my forthcoming book. (If you're interested in further and deeper reflection at this stage of your Race to Amazing, go to www.your10yearoldself.com and download a full reflections questionnaire to prompt your memory and help with further self-discovery.)

Another way to break down your lifeline exercise for greater understanding is to look at your talents, gifts, and inherent skills. What were you born with? What's in your DNA? Overlay that with your life experiences, your family dynamics, where you grew up, the type of schools you went to, and the friends you made. Lastly, look at your learned behaviors. This may be through education and development or career experiences.

Then take a moment to list the top three in each of these areas:

Inherent skills/talents/gifts

1.
2.
3.

Unique life experiences

1.
2.
3.

Learned/developed behavior/education

1.
2.
3.

• •

The combination of all of the above has created you. After understanding yourself better and knowing what you want to accomplish, you can be very deliberate and intentional about identifying key learning objectives, and then creating a developmental plan to get there. This book will put you on the fast track to reaching your goals and making the life changes you need.

In a few chapters you'll be on the Race to Amazing business track, and will hear more about "playing big" from a position of strength. Until then, remain focused on personal reflection and discovering more about you. Are you "playing big" from your position of strength? Maybe you know your personal strengths and weaknesses, and you're in a position or career where you're able to use your talents daily. If that's the case, then you're highly effective, enjoy your work, feel fulfilled, accomplished, and are already well on your Race to Amazing. If the above doesn't describe you, and how you're feeling right now, don't be discouraged. For many of us it can take a lifetime to understand who we are at our core, and to live our life with greater purpose and meaning.

For me, well, it took twenty years.

Discover Your Strengths

 After high school, I attended Clarion University of Pennsylvania and majored in special education. It wasn't my chosen school or major, but it's what I was told to do, because that was where my cousin went to college, and that's the degree she got. I'm not at all knocking her. She was on the right path. Today, she is Dr. Karen (Pickles) Taylor, a very accomplished teacher, principal, professor, and consultant.

I took a Speech 101 class my freshman year, for an easy A. I had competed in high school with the forensic team and won first place at a Pennsylvania State Championship for persuasive speech, so I decided to pull that speech out of the bag for the first speech delivery. That moment changed the course of my life.

My professor pulled me aside afterward and asked me to consider changing my major to communications. In exchange, he would mentor and counsel me over the next four years (definitely a high point at age twenty on my lifeline). He did just that. For the next four years I was actively involved in my major, gained as much learning and experience as I could handle, and discovered my strengths.

Another result of all the great mentoring I received was getting to be a sports broadcaster. I loved being one of the first female sports broadcasters on Clarion University's Sports Center 5. Next, for three years I co-hosted Community Update, a live weekly TV show, where I interviewed local businesses and leaders on soft news in the community. Being the female voice-over for radio commercials for Magic 96, in Brookville, Pennsylvania, took me out of the university environment and into the real broadcasting world. This led to my being master of ceremonies for the Miss Pennsylvania pageant, and for the live broadcast of the Autumn Leaf Parade my senior year.

I was so fortunate at twenty-two to have had the experiences I did, and to be so certain about my future career path. With my professor's mentorship and guidance, I was at a high point at graduation and ready to be the next Barbara Walters.

As luck or fate would have it, I moved to St. Louis in search of a big break in a larger market. Frustrated with many interviews and no offers, I accepted a desk job as a customer service rep, which spring-boarded my twenty-five-year sales career. I moved to Virginia and Chicago to open up offices for them and then got acquired by Boise Cascade Office Products (BCOP), now operating as OfficeMax/Office Depot.

I left BCOP in 1998 to take on my next big project as VP of Sales for a small woman-owned technology startup. Within six months, I was recruited back into the office products industry by Corporate Express (later acquired by Staples), as the VP of Sales for the South Atlantic Region. This was a big career step for me, as I was now responsible for ten sales managers and one hundred sales reps throughout North Carolina, South Carolina, and southern Virginia.

There's no way I would've been qualified, nor would I have had the courage to take on this role, if I hadn't been on the path of personal development with proven success. This role certainly came with many challenges, as we were dealing with mergers, acquisitions, new computer systems, realigning, consolidating, displacing employees, and trying to grow profitability quickly to meet the demands of the shareholders. I found myself often taking my eye off the ball of leadership development and coaching others, and would fall into the old patterns of just directing others what to do, and helping to close deals. But over time, our leadership team was able to take one of the lowest performing distribution centers in the company and turn it into one of the most respected and profitable locations in the country.

I've always been a firm believer that things happen for a reason. In life we face challenges, learn lessons, and have chance encounters that collectively help us discover who we are and enlighten us as to our true purpose. As I look back on my lifeline and career, I see a collective pattern that has made me who I am today. I remember my father being my biggest supporter, telling me, "You can do anything you put your mind to. You're a Shaffer (my family name)," as he was introducing me to those Jim Rohn motivational cassette tapes.

Later in life, I recall always wanting to take on the next big project or challenge, even if it required moving myself and my family around the country. I attribute my courage and motivation to my Grandma Betty, who said years ago when I was frustrated in corporate America, "You should just put your name on a business card and go sell yourself."

I remember the events of August 2002 like it was yesterday. I was driving to work after a long weekend at the beach with friends and family. But rather than feeling refreshed and relaxed, my stomach was in knots and my mind was racing. Something wasn't right. I had been thinking a lot about my purpose, my happiness, and my career. I was feeling unmotivated, uninspired, and unchallenged, and yearning for something more. I needed to fill a void in my soul and feed my desire to be happier. My relationship with my boss was deteriorating as my core values of trust, respect, and professionalism were being compromised. Over the years, I had lost respect for him. My mentor, who was his boss, was no longer with the company, which added to making our relationship tenuous.

That day in August, during my forty-minute road trip into the office, I turned off the radio and drove in complete silence. I began questioning my career path and whether I wanted to continue to devote my time and energy to that company. I had recently been nominated for a Leadership Succession Planning Program that would move me in a different direction and open up doors for career advancement. Why wasn't I excited about that? I felt like I just didn't want to work so hard—for them.

On the outside, I appeared to have it all together: a successful career, a happy family, and a loving marriage. But appearances can be deceiving. My two girls were having difficulty acclimating to adolescence, and needed me more than ever as I was absent for much of their formative years. I was worried about my father, who suffered from emphysema and was then on life support in the Intensive Care Unit in a nearby VA hospital. My twenty-year marriage was on the rocks. I didn't have it all together, but, more importantly, I knew that in order for my situation to change, I could no longer just wish things were different or blame others for my circumstances. I needed to change. But driving to work that morning, I had no idea that I would start the process so soon.

My boss called me into his office that morning and questioned something I had done. As I began to explain the situation, he got up from behind his desk, walked over, slammed the door, and told me to shut up and sit down. At that moment, I felt trapped, afraid, and frozen in time, unable to listen to anything that was being said to me. When I left his office, I left the building and never went back.

I quit my corporate job without another job lined up, and had no idea what I was going to do to earn an income. Since I had been so focused on my career for so many years and was the major breadwinner in the family, it was quite a shock to everyone.

However, the ride home that day was invigorating. The convertible top was down. I was free, free to be me! I remember saying to myself, "If you want things to change, then you have to change." I felt guilty that I was feeling so happy and excited about the future. I was going to create and build something, and this time do it on my own and my way. I just didn't know what it was, yet.

My life changed the day that I walked out of my corporate job without a career lined up. Although it was an overdue change, I was ready to focus on something challenging and new but wanted it to be right for me and for my family. In the long run, I wanted to win. What the winning meant for me was to discover my strengths and life purpose, to use my God-given talents and give back to others while building a business, yet making time for what really matters most: to love, spend time with, and enjoy my family and friends.

I began to reflect on my many years working for corporate America, and the sacrifices that I made for my girls and my family. I began asking myself, "What do I love? What am I great at? What would I love to do every day, even if I didn't get paid? What are my biggest regrets, and how can I ensure that I don't have them again?" I began to look closely at what I truly enjoyed the most about my job responsibilities and experiences over my career. It certainly wasn't all the travel, the stress, or working nights and weekends. I knew for sure it wasn't the rush to meet deadlines or sitting in front of the CEO trying to justify the numbers. No, I hated that.

What I did love though were the people, especially helping and watching them grow and develop, personally and professionally. I loved being able to take what I've learned about effective leadership and intentionally applying it to see the impact it could have on others. I loved strategic thinking, the challenge of a startup and building something new. I was at my peak when asked to move to a new location, lead a new concept or idea, or build a fresh new territory or team. But mostly, I loved the rewarding feeling of helping others learn and grow and making a difference in someone else's life.

I then looked at what was missing over those years and questioned if I was using my talents to the best of my ability. This was the first time I asked myself a powerful question that gave me tremendous insights, "What were you doing when you were ten?" Through that process, I realized how much I love to write, and at age ten I was making up stories and writing in my journal every day. The only writing I did in the corporate world was proposals and emails. When I was ten, I would read books out loud standing in front of the mirror, articulating every word. I recalled my love for public speaking, and the wonderful feeling of engaging and motivating large audiences. I remembered winning my high school and college speech competitions, and how comfortable I was hosting live television talk shows. In corporate America, I was often asked *not* to speak (or told to shut up and sit down, for that matter) or had to choose my words very carefully.

Along with this intense self-reflection, I searched and prayed, trying to fit all the pieces together to discover what I wanted to do with my next forty years. This mental preparation and planning was essential before I could begin my Race to Amazing.

K.Coaching, Inc. was born from all that research and self-reflection. It was fifteen years ago that I made the shift and began releasing my entrepreneurial spirit while building an executive coaching, consulting, and training organization. I had been preparing my entire life for that, so it was a natural fit. I'm now writing daily, coaching fabulous leaders, and helping businesses leaders discover their strengths and grow in competitive markets. I get to address and motivate audiences through speaking engagements and telling my story, to help others discover their strength and achieve success in their personal lives and their careers. The greatest reward is freedom. I'm still free to be me and can take the time I need for my family and friends.

I share my journey with you, because your Race to Amazing begins with the end in mind and requires awareness of your current state and what is missing or what needs to change. Shortly after I left my job, I left my husband of twenty years. Now these are significant, life-altering changes and I'm certainly not suggesting that you need to make such drastic or bold moves. The point is, it was at a time when I lightened my load, and this gave me space to be more reflective, to take time to fully understand where I was and where I wanted to go. When I was down, it was much quieter and I could begin to understand and see things more clearly. My windshield became clean, and I learned how important it is to have my antenna up and a clear vision in order to move forward.

CHAPTER 3—
LEADERSHIP ASSESSMENT

"Good character isn't formed in a week or a
month. It is created little by little. Protracted and patient
effort is needed to develop good character."

—Heraclitus

Leaders Create Leaders

Over the years, I've been fortunate to meet and work with some wonderful people and inspiring leaders who have been willing to help me succeed. I would often seek out mentors who would take me under their wing, while helping me pave a path for advancement. They would remove obstacles, keep their eyes open for developmental projects, and truly have a personal investment and concern for my future. These amazing leaders got to know me personally, while showing me they cared and understood what was important to me. They identified areas for my further development and challenged me with stretch assignments, while inspiring me to achieve.

These same types of mentors, coaches, and influencers are out there for you. Seek them out. True leaders create future leaders. When you evolve into a truly inspirational leader, you'll become aware of how your actions influence those who work for you. You'll then want to give back and directly mentor and support other aspiring leaders' careers as well. Doing this will make a huge difference in your life for giving back makes you doubly blessed and is a reward in and of itself.

There is no question, in my career as a sales executive, and dealing with mergers and acquisitions, I experienced a mishmash of leadership styles, cultures, and management systems. I witnessed first-hand the leadership style of some of the most ego-driven, emotionally unintelligent jerks as well. They were clueless about the impact they would have on others' sense of self-worth, motivation, and drive. Now I'm not saying they were all bad guys or necessarily terrible leaders—just unaware and therefore unable to change or control their behavior. It's because of those bad bosses and from those uncomfortable encounters and negative experiences that I may have learned the most. I learned more about what *not* to do, how *not* to act, as I experienced firsthand how degraded their behavior can make others feel.

Even if you're a highly skilled and successful leader today, think about these next exercises as a way to further discover leadership characteristics, and focus on your strengths and purpose. No one is perfect, and you may learn things that will help validate who you know you already are or provide insights into areas that you can further develop. You may also consider using some of these activities for your own purposes, such as team building, receiving feedback, or using this as part of performance reviews or developmental planning for your employees.

These examples and discovery activities are designed to create self-awareness around your current leadership style, where your current leadership style might have come from, and how others perceive you. Remember my first client, Dave? At first he was unprepared for coaching and could not recognize the need for it. Once you become fully aware, you can set your own course and create your developmental plan. This is a key element in *Race to Amazing*, and if done properly, it will put you on the fast track to reaching your goals, and making the life changes you desire.

Reflection Activity

Send a text to close friends, family, and colleagues, asking them what they think your superpower is. These are your natural, unique, and powerful strengths.

Make a list of the common superpower themes.

Where do you get your energy?

What drains your energy?

Next take a moment and do some quiet, personal reflection on who you are today as a leader.

Describe your leadership style. How would your business partner(s) or peer manager(s) describe you?

What would your direct reports say they'd like you to change in order to be more effective?

• •

Others' Perceptions

You've heard the adage "perception is reality." This means regardless of what's real, the way others view you or perceive you may ultimately be what matters most. Unfortunately, someone's perception or opinion of you can be formed by an accidental event or moment when they observed something about you and made a judgment.

In some cases, they may have heard a story about you and formed their own opinion, or were influenced by someone else's recollection or interpretation.

For example, if someone sees you every day, but has very little interaction with you, they may form an opinion based on what they observe from afar: how you dress, how you walk, or how you interact with others. If you tend to always be rushing to and fro with an intense look on your face, and keep your door shut throughout the day, how will others perceive you? They might think that you're disheveled, unorganized, unhappy, or unapproachable. If others observe you walking around the office with a smile on your face, stopping to have a brief, caring conversation with others, you'll more likely be perceived as being in control, pleasant, positive, and interested.

Others' perceptions of you will be closer to reality if they come from your boss, direct reports, or peers who have interacted with you on a daily or weekly basis. In addition, their opinions will be derived from their experiences, interactions, and observations of you over time. These are the individuals you'll have the most influence over. But the perception of others who don't know you very well will either contribute to a bad reputation or a tremendous followership.

360 Evaluations

One of the best ways my team and I have helped leaders understand how others perceive their performance and leadership style is through 360 evaluations. These are conducted in the form of an online survey, where participants are asked a series of questions, ranking the leader in question based on his or her leadership characteristics and effectiveness. There is also a free-form comment section included, so participants can expand their thoughts and offer examples.

Then once the participants have completed the survey, the results are summarized and analyzed by their assigned coach. This assessment enables the coach to better understand others' perception of the leader they'll be working with, and prepares them for the Race to Amazing coaching engagement.

The term *360* references all the relationships that are part of your full circle of influence. As a result, it's very important to have the right sampling of people and positions filling out the assessment. For example, you don't want to give this only to your direct reports, but rather, share it with a cross-functional group that may have a direct or indirect relationship with you. We tend to say, "The more the merrier," because once the insights, comments, and data are collected, we can draw a better analysis. We do this by viewing the results based on the type of relationships and interactions one has had with the leader being reviewed along with the length of time the participant has worked with him or her.

The survey questions are designed to receive insights or ranking of leadership effectiveness and are aligned with various high-performing leadership characteristics. These characteristics are then scored from an opinion scale, and can be benchmarked against other team members, companies, or similar job designs. Finally, the results of the 360 evaluation enable the coach to identify common themes and help the leader identify coaching objectives. It's not the only tool used, but it's a proven method for gathering opinions, ranking leaders against high-performing leadership characteristics, creating awareness, and gaining commitment to leadership development.

Confidential Environment

In order for us to gather honest feedback, participants need to know that their individual scoring and comments will be confidential and won't be shared with the leader they're evaluating. They should also be made aware that common themes will be gathered and shared with the leader, but the leader will not know who specifically said what in the comment section of the assessment results.

High-Performance Leadership Characteristics

In this section are examples and descriptions of high-performance leadership characteristics. This is a collection of what we see as consistent, proven qualities of highly effective leaders who motivate high-performing businesses, high-impact teams, and high-potential individuals. The 360 evaluation would typically have five to six questions that align with each of these leadership characteristics. The combination of scores from the individual questions creates the average score for that particular characteristic.

Top Twelve High-Performance Leadership Characteristics

Take a look at the following characteristics and think about how others might rank you on a frequency scale of 1 to 4. Write that number in the square provided.

1. Never 2. Sometimes 3. Frequently 4. Always

☐ **Adaptability**

Modifies and adjusts their leadership style based on the needs of others to maximize results.

☐ **Empathy**

Emotionally connects, identifies with, and understands others' feelings, culture, or situation.

☐ **Vision, mission, and strategy (Communications)**

Provides the big picture for the organization and its leaders. Then creates the strategic plans, communicates and leads effectively while achieving the desired results.

☐ **Feedback (Communications)**

Provides a balance of constructive and positive feedback in an appropriate way, to motivate continued behavior or inspire change.

☐ **Coaching style (Communications)**

Actively listens, questions, and understands, rather than directing and telling.

☐ **Predictability**

Leads and communicates in a manner that is consistent, expected, and understood by everyone.

Trust

Does what they say they're going to do. Shows genuine interest in others' success. Displays sincerity and integrity.

 Self-awareness

Understands the impact of their actions, behavior, and leadership style on others, and what they need to change to be most effective.

☐ **Emotional control**

Demonstrates emotional maturity. Withholds emotional responses until processed in a logical way. Responds appropriately, rather than reacting to situations and others.

☐ **Fair**

Treats others equally and with respect, without showing favoritism or being pushy with their position.

 Motivating

Identifies motivating factors in others and inspires them to be the best they can be.

☐ **Relationship focus**

Acts proactively and intentionally to build relationships with customers, employees, and business partners.

• •

Now that you've spent some time reflecting on your current leadership style, gaining the opinions and perceptions of others, and score-boarding yourself against high-performance leadership characteristics, you should be well on your way to being self-aware and ready to set your course.

Think of this as your Personal Course Plan for becoming intentional and deliberate about what you're going to focus on, based on what you discovered and what you'd like to change. But know that your plan may shift throughout the race, as you gain insights and learn more about how to improve your high-performance leadership characteristics.

As an executive and business coach, I've discovered many common themes and roadblocks that can impede successful leadership. Throughout *Race to Amazing*, I'll share success stories and best practices of high-performance leaders, along with proven successful sales management systems. You may see new methods, fresh ideas, or approaches that you want to try yourself or implement with your own team and company.

Once you create your Personal Course Plan, you'll create an accountability system for yourself. This will also make it easier to recognize and identify key topics and particular chapters that will resonate and best align with your developmental plan.

Personal Course Plan

Review the reflections activity, others' perceptions, and your scores on the High-Performance Leadership Characteristics in this chapter. Determine your top three leadership development areas and list them below.

 Your Top Three Leadership Development Areas

1.

2.

3.

If your personal Race to Amazing is successful, what changes would be made or what skills gained?

How will you, your team, or your company benefit from the achievement of your program objective(s)?

How will you know if you've been successful with your Race to Amazing?

What will be the checkpoints along the way?

CHAPTER 4—GOOD BOSS, BAD BOSS

"Management is doing things right;
leadership is doing the right things."

—Peter F. Drucker

As a business coach, I'm often asked the difference between a successful, growing, thriving business, and one that is stagnant, tired, and slow to change or grow. Does the difference lie in its investment in technology, their people, their marketing, or their great service? These are all likely contributors, but I can sum up the principle source of the difference in one word: leadership.

You can have the latest advancements in technology, the best people onboard, and money to invest in systems and processes, but without effective leadership, you may have nothing. Most people who are in a leadership role truly want to be great at what they do, but they're not getting the business growth and the results they're hoping for. It is common for those people to look at all of the potential causes of slow growth, but they don't often look within and recognize what they could do better or different to affect their team's success.

They might not be aware that they have fallen into a pattern of bad habits, or have limited exposure to what a truly effective leadership style looks like. More often than not, leaders tend to wear many hats, and work long, hard hours directly in the business, rather than working on thinking strategically about the business.

When I'm working with coaching clients that seem to be falling into this trap, we address the first hurdle to becoming a better leader. This hurdle involves gaining a clear understanding of the difference between management and leadership. Because this is such a common occurrence, I believe that everyone benefits from the practice of reviewing the fundamentals of management versus leadership.

Keep in mind that leadership isn't a position, but an evolving set of actions. Just because you have the title—business owner, president, CEO, vice president of sales, sales manager—doesn't mean you're a leader. First, it's important to identify the skills you naturally possess, assess your comfort zones, and target the areas where you may need to improve to be a more effective leader *and* manager.

A great description of the difference is, managers manage "things," and leaders lead "people." Many of you might be thinking, "I do both." If you manage people and processes, you're a manager and a leader, and you have a very important job.

Management vs. Leadership

Management is more about planning, organizing, staffing, directing, and measuring. Those tasks may include creating the internal systems and processes, developing plans, quota setting, measuring and monitoring performance, giving feedback, and holding people accountable.

Leadership, on the other hand, is the ability to translate vision into reality. The leader must be a guide, a person who leads others along the way. In business, a leader guides through honesty, thinking strategically, and communicating effectively. A leader is also inspiring and motivating, yet empathic, humble, and caring.

• •

Comparison Activity

The Management vs. Leadership comparison activity, below, will help you to better understand how much of your time you're spending on management versus leadership activities.

Rank yourself on a scale of **one to five** (with one being the lowest) on each of the following management descriptors, then add up your scores.

Management

	1	2	3	4	5
Day-to-Day Focus					
Establishing a Plan					
Problem Solving					
Organizing the Details					
Staffing					
Communicating Plans					
Monitoring & Reinforcing					
Implementing Plans					
Managing Change					
Delegating					

Score: _____ total points out of 50 possible points

Now rank yourself on a scale from **one to five** (with one being the lowest) on each of the following leadership descriptors, then add up your scores.

Leadership

	1	2	3	4	5
Being Future-Oriented					
Establishing a Vision					
Employing Strategic Thinking					
Seeing the Big Picture					
Team Building					

Communicating the Vision					
Inspiring and Energizing					
Removing Barriers					
Being a Change Agent					
Coaching/Supporting					

Score: _____ total points out of 50 possible points

• •

There truly is a difference between management and leadership. Remember, a leader leads people and a manager manages things, which are both important roles in any organization. We will be addressing management skills, sales management systems, and processes in greater detail in upcoming chapters.

Utilize your score to continue and build on your strengths, while identifying opportunities to work on any "gaps." You may even go back and add to your Personal Course Plan.

It's also not uncommon for entrepreneurs or small business owners to play a sales manager or sales leadership role within their organization. When coaching small businesses, we often hear that the owner is spending more time working "in their business," rather than "on their business." If this is the case for you, it's likely you have a much higher management score. You may discover that it will require shifting your time to vision-casting, strategic thinking, or delegating.

Your role as a manager and your position as a leader are critical to the overall success of the organization. In fact, your management and leadership style could make or break the success of your company and your employees. If you found a gap between the management and leadership descriptors, and need to focus more of your time on leadership activities, ask yourself the following reflection questions and make a commitment to change.

• •

Reflection Questions

 In my current role, am I more of a leader or a manager? Why?

What areas can I work on to be seen more as a leader than a manager?

What specific changes do I need to make?

Categories of Leaders

Leadership styles have certainly evolved. When I think back over my career, the leadership styles were very different from what we see today. Quite frankly, leaders got away with a lot more than they would now. I remember working for someone who would get so angry that his face would turn red. He would start yelling profanities and then seemingly turn into the Incredible Hulk! He could empty a room in seconds as employees left feeling scared. All of this acting out was because his employees weren't doing what he asked them to do.

Leadership studies reveal a leadership continuum, reflecting on how past and future leaders treat their employees and handle certain situations. The shift in leadership styles aligns clearly with the shift in business culture, which focuses on involving more employees in business decision-making, rather than forced directives. Now the focus is on the culture, treating employees with respect, and motivating and inspiring others to succeed. Leadership is no longer seen as just a position or title, but rather as actions and influence.

Democratic vs. Autocratic Leaders

Democratic leaders emerged, leaving the autocratic "old-school" leader behind. For the most part, the autocratic leader tends to be more task-oriented, directive, and authoritative, and not as effective as the more evolved democratic leader. The democratic leader is more supportive, collaborative, and relationship oriented. Following are examples of the differences in behavior between an autocratic and a democratic leader.

Autocratic Leaders

☐ Not engaged unless something is wrong, then they speak up.

☐ Uninterested in others' ideas; considers their own ideas the right ones or the only ones.

☐ Hold information or knowledge close to their vest.

☐ Sporadically change direction or demands.

☐ Aloof, unapproachable, and hard to talk to.

☐ Discourage people from trying new things or taking risks.

☐ Determine performance standards without the input of others.

Democratic Leaders

☐ Consider others' ideas, even if they conflict with their own.

☐ Allow a reasonable margin of error, without being overly critical.

☐ Try to help others learn from their mistakes.

☐ Maintain high expectations and provide opportunities.

☐ Help people understand the objectives and specific tactics for success in their jobs.

☐ Set goals and objectives *with* people, rather than directing.

As leadership styles are evolving in most companies, it's not uncommon to find that certain organizations and cultures still reflect the autocratic leadership style. This may be prevalent in small, family-owned businesses where the leadership culture and management methods were created, and still exist, from previous generations.

The new generation of democratic leaders may be slower to shift the culture in manufacturing and production facilities that hold onto strong management traditions that are job-centered and task-oriented. Also, certain organizations, such as those that need a quick turnaround or swift reorganization, may require more of an authoritative leadership style.

When it's difficult to make this shift or certain leaders are steadfast in how they believe leadership should be, it's important to look at what employees say they need from their leader. Understanding what employees want and need from their leader can provide insight into what is really important to them. Having this understanding can provide leaders with a few reminders of what they may need to be more conscious of in order to satisfy their employees' needs and ultimately get better results.

Consider the following results of a Harvard Business Review study, where they asked employees what they wanted from their leader. The following responses were provided, in this order:

1. "Share your vision: what do you want us to accomplish?"
2. "Tell us how you think we are doing."

3. "Tell us how our team is doing and where we fit into the bigger picture."
4. "Show us that you care."

On the surface, these seem like realistic and doable actions that you as a leader can ensure you have in your repertoire every day. But day-to-day business can often take over and you may forget about what's really important, such as how employees feel about you and what they want from you, their leader. If you were an employee who didn't receive these types of things from your leader, how motivated would you be?

When employees were asked to further provide feedback on how a leader can show they care, they stated that being appreciated by their boss was number one. A leader can certainly show appreciation with simple words such as, "Thank you," or saying, "I really appreciate the work you're doing." Even so, these platitudes can sometimes feel insincere, and may not be taken seriously.

Appreciative Susan

 Susan is a sales leader for a business-to-business services company. She is responsible for $15 million in revenue, and manages five sales executives and three customer service representatives. On paper, the team was at 97.5 percent of their quota for the year, and projected to be on track to reach 100 percent by year end. After receiving the results of her 360 evaluation, it was apparent that the employees felt she was aloof, seemingly too busy, and they often felt their contributions were taken for granted. Susan was very surprised by the feedback, because she would continuously tell them "Thank you," and that she appreciated their work. Through our coaching conversations, she discovered that her kind words were routine and likely perceived as just good manners, rather than meaningful. What they really wanted was more of her attention and to feel appreciated. Together, Susan and I worked on carving out more one-on-one time for her sales reps and having better communication with the customer service team about the company's success, while including an incentive or rewards program.

On average, Susan was spending two to three days a week in the field working with her sales reps, but she recognized it was not quality time. She found herself rushing to and from appointments, taking phone calls in between, and often complaining to sales reps about her workload and how busy she was. Next, Susan instituted a new schedule that ensured that she had an extra hour built-in for each scheduled appointment. This guaranteed that she would spend thirty minutes of one-on-one time with each sales rep, helping them with pre-planning and better preparation for appointments. Afterward, Susan would have thirty minutes of uninterrupted time to debrief them on the customer meeting. As a result of her new plan, she not only learned more about the business, but also guaranteed that her sales reps would feel that she truly cared about their success, and valued spending time with them.

Although, Susan initially thought squeezing this extra time into her day would be a daunting task, she recognized right away how worthwhile it was. Susan saw measurable results by creating quality time that would directly drive sales rep performance and improve sales.

Susan also wanted to address the customer service team, as they were feeling unappreciated after all of the hard work that they did to support the sales efforts. Susan even received feedback that the customer service team felt that she liked the sales team more than them. We reflected on the HBR study and coached around what the customer service reps wanted and needed from her and what was missing. She decided to communicate more with the customer service team about the company's direction, revenue, and profitability goals. If the sales team met their quotas, Susan offered an additional monthly bonus to the customer service team as a reward for their support.

When you look back at the HBR study and the four things that employees said they wanted from their leader, these new efforts would satisfy all four. These small changes in how Susan communicated and managed her time and her team made a direct impact on the success they achieved.

By the end of the year, the customer service team:

- Was fully engaged in supporting customers.
- Had a better understanding of their goals.
- Knew what and how they were doing.
- Understood where they fit into the big picture.

All the while, they were being rewarded accordingly. The sales team was getting more appointments, meeting their quota, and improving their skills because of the time and attention that Susan was now providing them. This resulted in them being at 109 percent of their plan for the year.

The steps Susan took as a result of both leadership awareness and the creation of her Personal Course Plan included:

- Taking to heart the feedback that she received on her 360 evaluation.
- Making changes in her management and leadership style, for both the sales team and the customer service team, recognizing that they had different needs even though they had similar complaints.
- Accepting coaching and taking the time to work on her own development.
- Putting a plan in place that made changes in her own style and approach
- Sticking to her plan.

Show You Care

Involving employees in the planning stages, rather than merely implementing decisions other people make, is the second most popular way bosses show they care. If this isn't common practice for you today, it may be as simple as arranging a brainstorming meeting and doing a SWOT analysis with your team as you're planning for a new quarter or planning your sales strategy for a new year. Some sales organizations have their sales representatives present to management what they believe their quotas or territory plan should be for the upcoming year.

This gives them a sense of ownership of their goals, makes them feel involved in the planning, and they appreciate it more than having a number handed down to them from their boss. In my experience, when organizations allow salespeople to come up with their own quotas and territory plans, their goals are often higher than the goals the company may have provided them. It gives you a great opportunity to meet them somewhere in between and gain their respect for how you're setting expectations and managing their performance.

Another way employees believe a leader demonstrates they care is by showing empathy and concern. That doesn't mean that you need to try to get on a deep personal level with your employees in order to be empathetic. Empathy is one of the key, high-performance leadership characteristics, and often the most difficult one to actually learn or teach.

If empathy is one area you want to address in your Race to Amazing Personal Course Plan, I suggest practicing understanding, listening more intently, and thinking with your heart in combination with your head. This takes practice!

Empathy with Jane

 Jane comes into your office sobbing. She is upset because she hasn't met her goals for the month and her commission check isn't going to be enough to pay her bills that month. Some leaders may not really be listening to what she has to say, because they're thinking about how she hasn't been making enough sales calls, has been coming to work late, and leaving early. What did she expect? She deserves this. Maybe you even hand her a tissue, and tell her how you feel. This is an autocratic leadership style.

The empathetic leader will ask questions to better understand what her situation is to try to connect with how she's really feeling, rather than just thinking that she's too emotional and needs to stop crying.

When the leader is empathetic, they're able to get to the root cause because they're listening with their heart. What the empathetic leader might discover is that Jane is under extreme stress at home because her mother is ill. Jane needs to be at the hospital early in the morning to feed her breakfast and at night for dinner. This is causing her a lot of stress and anxiety and has affected her work during that month.

When you truly understand how the other individual is thinking and feeling, you'll be able to connect with them on a deeper level that will enhance your ability to make the right decisions as it relates to them. Jane on the other hand, is going to feel as though you took the time to listen, care about her, and fully understand her current circumstance. That in itself is a motivator for her.

Good Boss vs. Bad Boss

One way to understand how to adjust your style is to be aware of what good leadership versus bad leadership actually looks like. The Good Boss vs. Bad Boss Activity, below, offers a great way to brainstorm the characteristics of leadership, and to better understand the impact that you can have on others, both positive and negative.

• •

Good Boss vs. Bad Boss Activity

 Take a moment and think about the different leaders that you've worked for, or with, in the past. Were they inspiring? What was it about them that made them an awesome leader? What were their specific characteristics? Conversely, recall a time when you may have been demotivated by a manager or someone in a leadership role. What did they do, or not do, that may have caused you to dislike them?

In the blocks below, list the characteristics that come to mind for a good boss versus a bad boss.

Good Boss vs. Bad Boss

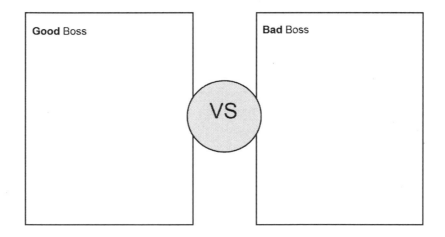

What are the top three characteristics that you want to be perceived as having?

1.
2.
3.

Now, write beside them what you can do to improve on that characteristic.

Example: <u>Good Listener</u> *I will turn away from my computer or cell phone when someone comes into my office to ask a question or to talk. I will demonstrate that they have my full attention by my body language and eye contact.*

Next, go back to the two lists and circle bad boss descriptors that someone may have used to describe you at one time or another. Then write down in the space below the specific actions or behaviors that you want to ensure you *do not* portray.

Example: <u>Unpredictable</u> *I will think before I act; responding rather than reacting emotionally, to ensure that I'm more consistent in my behavior.*

• •

Below is one of my favorite illustrations of the difference between a bad boss and an effective leader. There are many variations of this comparison, but we use this rendition with our coaching clients.

Take the time to thoughtfully read through the illustration, highlighting the ones that really resonate with you. Quite often clients will identify the bad boss as someone that they know or they've worked for in the past. It is important that you're honest with yourself and identify any bad boss characteristics that you may have.

- The bad boss drives their teams; the leader coaches them.
- The bad boss inspires fear; the leader inspires enthusiasm.
- The bad boss says "I"; the leader says "We."
- The bad boss says "Go"; the leader says "Let's go."
- The bad boss uses people; the leader develops them.
- The bad boss never has enough time; the leader makes time for things that count.
- The bad boss is concerned with things; the leader is concerned with people.
- The bad boss lets their people know where "I" stand; the leader lets their people know where "they" stand.
- The bad boss works hard to produce; the leader works hard to help their people produce.
- The bad boss takes credit; the leader gives it.

Preparing to be an amazing leader requires you to step back and be self-aware before you can move forward. Understanding the differences between management and leadership can help you begin to level up your strategic thinking and show you where to best spend your time.

Understanding the differences between good boss and bad boss characteristics can also help you self-assess your leadership style, further ensuring that you're not "that guy." For now, let's get comfortable with what amazing leadership looks like for *you*, and what actions you can take to be an amazing leader.

CHAPTER 5—MISSION, VISION, PASSION

"Good business leaders create a vision,
articulate the vision, passionately own the vision,
and relentlessly drive it to completion."

—Jack Welch

Mission, vision, and passion: these are the three words that form a foundation for sustainable success. Leaders will sometimes go straight for the strategy, or specific goals that need to be met, often not realizing how important it is that the mission, vision, and passion (MVP) come first.

Without direction or a clear path, how can you align strategy and tactics? How can you expect others to follow you if they're confused, not clear on what the true mission is, or what the future looks like for themselves and their company?

When working with executives, we discover one of two things. Either the mission and vision are not clear to the leader themselves because they have not established it in their own mind or on paper. Or the mission and vision of the company have been established, but not well disseminated or communicated with passion and conviction in order to ensure that there is execution and implementation by others.

MVP is one of the high-performance leadership characteristics which is defined as: The big picture is clearly communicated for the organization or team, outlines strategic plans, and passionately leads results through others. When sales leaders are having a difficult time building their sales strategy or creating their go-to-market plans, I naturally ask questions around mission and vision, while trying to understand their passion for leading and executing. If this sounds like you, and MVP is something you want to refine, communicate, or build better as part of your Personal Course Plan, then now is the time to begin.

Mission and Vision

Every company, no matter its size, needs an articulated mission and vision as a source of direction. This clear and concrete statement will let both your employees and your customers know precisely what the organization stands for and where it's going. This then provides a compass for your leadership team to follow.

Defining a vision and creating a clear mission statement are crucial elements in your company's strategic planning. They're the basis for building your sales strategies and your tactical plan to meet your business goals. Let's explore the difference between your mission and your vision statements, how to create them, and the positive effects they can have on your business.

A simple analogy is: A vision statement propels the company toward some future goal or achievement, while a mission statement guides current, critical, strategic decision-making. Your mission statement should be short, memorable, and able to communicate what the company stands for in just a few words. It should reflect your organization's passion and encompass the needs of both the company and its customers. Often, the mission statement is an integral part of your branding strategy, and should ultimately serve as a guide for current and future decision-making.

There are many methods for writing mission statements. You can choose to invest in outside consultants and spend days or weeks crafting the statement, or spend some time brainstorming with thought leaders within your own company. There's also nothing wrong with doing it solo and then receiving feedback from others that you respect and admire. Regardless of the method that you choose, the most important thing is that it gets done.

Below are some additional tips to writing a mission statement:

- Define your ideal customer.
- Define your products or services clearly.
- Describe *why* customers should buy from you.

Begin to craft your mission statement by asking the following questions:

Why does your business exist?

What benefits or value do you bring to your customers?

How do your products or services differ from your competition?

What wants, needs, desires, pain, or problems do your products and services solve?

The vision statement, more than the mission statement, propels the company toward its future goal and sharpens the business focus. After the mission statement is complete, now it's time to think about the vision statement, by asking the following questions:

How are you going to get where you're going?

What does the end result look like?

. . . .

Communicate with Clarity

Communicating and sharing your vision with everyone in your company enhances employee morale, as they gain a clearer understanding of the company's direction and, most importantly, their particular role in pursuit of the organization's success. Additionally, with a clear vision, employees will better understand their responsibilities. They will also understand specific actions they can take to personally impact the company and its future growth. Everyone wants and needs to feel like a part of something bigger and also feel appreciated for their contributions. It's a fundamental human trait, and a key motivational factor of individual performance. Not surprisingly, this type of clarity goes a long way toward fostering a team-oriented environment that will help attract and retain your best people.

Key Communications to Consider

- **Ensure everyone is *clear*, that there are no misunderstandings.** Hold an "all-hands" meeting to launch the mission and vision, to ensure the message is communicated the same way to all employees. Post it on your website, make banners to display it throughout the office, and place it on the front of your building.

- **Coach your staff to identify with, and *own*, the mission and vision. In essence, your employees are the company, and its growth depends on their commitment.** They must adopt the company direction and values as their own. A great exercise for gaining employee investment in the vision is to include them in the creation of the statements, so that they become stakeholders in the future of the organization. Lead your teams in brainstorming sessions on what they or their department can do to impact the business results and transfer these ideas into individual actions.

- Inspire customers and employees to ***believe*** in and identify with your mission and vision. Avoid broad declarations like, "We will be the best in the world." Your statements must be honest, realistic, and comprised of obtainable goals.

- Once you've defined your mission and vision statements, it's time to begin building on them. Hold an off-site meeting, gathering together your thought leaders, supervisors, and managers. Guide them through discussions and processes for defining specific, strategic, and tactical activities your organization will have to perform to pursue your stated direction.

Passion

Building upon your mission and vision and keeping them top-of-mind for days, weeks, and years to come will require the "P," passion! As I shared above, per Jack Welch, "The good business leader passionately owns the vision and relentlessly drives it to completion."

Passion isn't something that you can just turn on or off. It's in your heart and soul, and others can see it as you demonstrate it through your actions and your words. It creates inspiration—the inspiration that others need from you as a leader. Your passion will set the tone for your company culture, your employees' mindset, and their attitudes. Creating inspiration through your passion as a leader is being able to express your *why*—why you do what you do.

Remember, nothing great in this world has ever happened without passion. It's up to you to find that passion and understand it so that you can live it, love it, and lead it.

Aussies with PUC

There are only a handful of times that I've seen, first-hand, the type of passion and commitment that most of us dream of having and displaying. I'd like to share with you a story of a business owner and his leadership team who I worked with nine years ago in Australia. Their passion, urgency, and commitment (PUC) were truly contagious.

Following an 8:00 a.m. arrival after a twenty-hour flight, a quick shower, and a taxi to Rydalmere, I joined the leadership team at Complete Office Supply (COS) in its new headquarters, located outside Sydney, Australia. I was brought there to work on strategic planning, and present at the company's national sales conference a few days later. I'd worked with similar successful companies in the United States in their industry, and was excited to share best practices.

Upon entering the meeting room, I immediately felt the energy, excitement, and a winning attitude that was absolutely infectious. My first thoughts were, "What is happening here? How do you get this kind of energy?" I figured they must be in a unique market or have minimal competition to be so self-assured, action-oriented, and committed to the company's success.

But I discovered quite the opposite. COS had aggressive competitors vying for their business, but they calmly focused on gaining market share while ensuring next-day delivery to businesses scattered over 3 million square miles.

We started the first day sharing ideas, successes, and best practices for competing and creating sustainable profitable business growth. We ended the day with a "Motivating Others" seminar that they took very seriously, implementing a number of the ideas immediately. What I saw in the first five hours was great leadership and fun-loving, hard-working, enthusiastic people with a clear vision and direction for their company. But what they knew best was how to carry that through with passion. In their conversations throughout the day they exhibited winning attitudes and showed me how to motivate others with passion, urgency, and commitment—what they referred to as "PUC"—and they lived it.

Energize Through Reward and Recognition

We all know how important reward and recognition is for motivation. I saw it demonstrated with their High Achievers Club, exclusive for those who met or exceeded their quotas for the year. They then had a day of surprise activities to recognize their achievements and the PUC it took to get there.

That day began with a one-hour speedboat ride on Sydney Harbor. Describing it as "fast" doesn't do this thrill ride justice! The seatbelts held back the high achievers as they put their hands in the air, as though on a roller coaster, while the speedboat did 360-degree turns, repeatedly reaching record speeds, before slamming on its brakes. Of course, when offered a wetsuit before boarding, no one accepted. That would have been for mates without PUC.

The second adventure took place at Center Point, the tallest building in Australia. High achievers were cable-strapped and led on an outdoor walk with a glass floor, 268 meters above Sydney. Not for the faint of heart or someone without PUC.

Their next stop was The Rocks and the Italian Village for one of the finest lunches in Sydney. Here, everyone met the sales managers, relaxed, enjoyed a cocktail or two, and happily ended their adventurous day. Or, so they thought. The conclusion of the gathering was unexpectedly rocked by the thunder of twenty-six Harley Davidson motorcycles lined up outside for these high achievers, who then took a motorcycle tour through the streets of Sydney. Escorted by Aussie bikers, they ventured up the coast to Bondi

Beach and then back to the hotel, just in time to get showered and dressed for the formal awards dinner.

This was a reward and recognition of the highest order. As the honored guests received their awards and gave their acceptance speeches, their quota against achievement was projected behind them, accompanied by a motivational theme song chosen by their manager. The other sales reps in the room were in awe and admiration, no doubt wondering how they might get more PUC so they could be a part of the club next year.

In many companies, the importance of recognition is often forgotten. During his acceptance speech, one high achiever said in appreciation of the great day and his award, "Thank you, it means a lot to me. I'm sure you've heard about recognition. Babies cry for it, men die for it."

Inspiring Leadership

On the tour bus, the CEO, Dominique Lyons, stood in front of his high achievers, shared his vision for growth, thanked them for their hard work, and congratulated them for their contribution and achievement. At the anniversary celebration, he stood on a new forklift with his four-year-old in his arms, addressing salespeople from across different states, sharing his vision for the future, his hopes for the new distribution center, and the growth opportunities for the company and for all of them.

Later, Dominique cut the anniversary cake and discussed his vision for the next thirty years and the goal of $100 million by 2010. He talked about how his family came to Australia when he was five years old with a dream of prosperity in a new country. As he spoke, I watched the faces of his employees and felt the energy and electricity of this organization and these people. I considered giving up my U.S. citizenship, leaving my children, and moving to Australia—just to work for him and COS. I felt the PUC; it was palpable. Now this, I thought, is inspiring leadership. PUC, I learned, has no boundaries and no limits. It could easily be the number one differentiator between a leader and an amazing sales leader.

Now, it's time to take your vision and mission and make great results happen. Sales leadership is all about your ability to turn a vision into reality. This happens when you build an effective go-to-market strategy that everyone can embrace and build passion around, so you too can lead your mission and vision. It's all about achieving PUC.

CHAPTER 6—PLAN TO WIN

"A satisfied customer is the best business strategy of all."

—Michael LeBoeuf

When it comes to building a successful go-to-market strategy, I pull from knowledge I gained through life experiences, including entering a new market as an independent start-up leader, and expanding markets as a sales leader for a Fortune 500 company. Often, these markets had declining sales, no market share, or poor name recognition. In both cases, the sales teams were new or needed retooling. Basically, these sales teams needed to be built from scratch.

 The first company I worked for grew to $100 million in ten years. Companies usually don't grow that fast or position themselves for an exit without having a strategy and plan. But, in the early days and as a frontline employee, it didn't feel very strategic.

I vividly remember the first day in my first sales position. I was totally clueless about what to do. My sales training was very simple, "Here's the phone. Go sell something." It didn't take me long to understand what the job entailed: make a lot of phone calls, get something to bid on, and win the business. In this case, I was selling computer and office supplies to the Federal Government, but it was more like, "We will find and sell them anything they want to buy."

Fortunately, in those days it was pretty easy to get the sale. There was no voicemail or email, fax machines weren't invented yet, and IBM had just come out with the first PC. When I made a phone call to ask for a chance to bid on something, 99 percent of the time I spoke to a live person who was warm and friendly, and willing to give me an opportunity.

Because I was dealing with the Federal Government, they needed three prices in order to compete against most of their larger bids. So, I would give them all three prices and would receive an order 60 percent of the time! What they did on their end, I have no idea.

As a twenty-four-year-old in my first real job out of college, I wasn't a strategic thinker. But thirty years later, older and wiser, I look back and remember the strong, competitive strengths and differentiators I had. As a sales team, we were focused on winning, every day. We were pioneers with a competitive edge. It was the new computer era, and we were selling hardware, software, printer supplies, and accessories to buyers who had little to no experience with these product categories. We had a niche; business was brisk, margins were high, and the competition was slim.

After a few years in telemarketing sales, I moved to Alexandria, Virginia, to expand the Federal Government business. It was 1988, during the Reagan years, and an exciting time to be working in Washington DC. I was twenty-seven, facing my first sales manager role, clearly a victim of being placed in management because I was a good salesperson. My sales management training was, "Hire people like you and show them the ropes."

It was there, through trial and error and living on PUC, that I learned my first lessons in leadership. We built an amazing team of successful salespeople and six years later we were at a $12 million run rate. It wasn't long after that I was asked to move to Chicago to open up an office. Déjà vu. No employees, no distribution center, no name recognition. It was time to start from scratch and build again, this time with a mission and a vision.

My direction was very clear. On day one, my boss said, "All I want you to do is go after Boise Cascade Office Products' customers and take the computer supplies business." One thing he did know about me is that I work well with very simple, clear direction, and a challenge. So that's what we did. I hired a team of great salespeople and we went into large corporate accounts, chipping away at Boise Cascade Office Products' accounts and relationships.

Within the first eight months, we landed a $4 million contract and the toner business for Walgreens pharmacies throughout North America; and yes, it was a Boise account. One year later, Boise Cascade Office Products acquired us. It didn't take me long after that to figure out that I was strategically placed in Chicago, just a few miles from Boise's headquarters, with a very clear go-to-market strategy, and a plan to get their attention.

It was through those early years working for a small company in sales and management, combined with working as a sales leader for Fortune 500 companies, that I was able to establish a successful go-to-market methodology. This is what we use today with hundreds of our current coaching and consulting clients.

As leaders and particularly sales leaders, you may have your own methodology for establishing a go-to-market plan. It really is a collection of great ideas, trial and error, and more importantly adapting to change and being flexible. So many businesses live on a hope and a dream, and for whatever reason, keep doing the same things over and over again, getting the same unsatisfactory results.

It is important to not mistake enthusiasm for strategy. The quintessential sales manager should certainly be enthusiastic with a positive attitude that is motivating and inspiring. But one must consider whether this is a mask for lack of confidence or clarity on what the vision, mission, and strategy is for the sales organization.

We've asked very capable sales managers about their strategy for the upcoming year and get lip service in return. Instead of concrete strategies and tactical plans we hear things like, "We're going to kick butt this year. Bring it on!" or worse, "Our plan is to bring in new accounts and grow the business!" Duh. Sorry, no real strategy here. We love the enthusiasm, but it just doesn't cut it. Without a clearly defined go-to-market strategy, there is nothing to lead, and you'll get lackluster results.

Building a go-to-market strategy is creating a strategic plan to proactively and intentionally gain market share. Ask yourself, what can you do better? What do you need to change or do different to get better results? And then, how do you execute that plan through others? For me, that is the essence of sales leadership.

I often meet with sales leaders and successful companies that on the surface seemingly have it altogether. But once we dig in, I would characterize them as (in nothing but the kindest way) "dysfunctionally successful." Just because they might have been successful for many years doesn't mean they have a sustainable methodology for sales strategy creation. Sometimes, it's just plain luck. Maybe it's the right industries at the right time, a high demand product, or staying ahead of the technology curve? We see companies that have been successful for many years suddenly realizing they've been riding a wave, and with no real go-to-market strategy. Now with major economic changes, greater and more aggressive competition, and customers spending less, they struggle with adapting to these changing circumstances. So now they may feel as though they need to reinvent themselves or become more intentional or strategic in their approach to growth.

Early in my career, as an inexperienced sales manager, I was certainly what you would call "dysfunctionally successful." For many years I approached my job each day with passion, commitment, and a positive attitude, which seemed to be enough to lead others.

Eventually, like many of you, I learned the hard way that this approach only gets you so far. It took me fifteen years to realize that there was a method behind all the madness. Once I could look back and connect the dots, I could see a tried-and-true approach to creating a go-to-market strategy, and where it worked.

I then understood the importance of hiring dedicated talent, and having motivated people. Also, I realized how absolutely necessary it is to have a clearly defined vision and then be able to communicate direction and expectations.

Since then, I've learned the importance of having a documented sales strategy and processes with an easy to implement management system. Above all, I've learned how important focus and leadership is to the execution of the plan, and actually making it happen!

Today, this methodology has helped K.Coaching move

hundreds of companies from "dysfunctionally successful" to strategically driven, with a growth plan that is motivating and will achieve the results they're looking for.

Methodology

The K.Coaching Sales Strategy Creation Model includes four basic elements – Discovery, Alignment, Implementation, and Leadership. This is a phased approach with Discovery and Alignment taking place first, resulting in the creation of a game plan. The second phase is Implementation and Leadership. This is the action and the execution phase. Unfortunately, Phase 2 is the more difficult of the two, and where leadership, generally, can make or break the strategy.

Discovery

This phase requires "thinking time," which many of us never seem to find. It's more than just a fleeting thought or a brilliant idea that comes from reading a book or watching a movie. I recall hating when a previous boss would take a business trip, because he would take the time on the plane to catch up on his business reading. He was notorious for coming back to the office with another new idea or flavor of the month. This isn't my definition of discovery.

Think of discovery as seeing or becoming aware of something for the first time. Uncovering through peeling back the onion, and seeing what is at the core of the business or the problem.

We suggest using the Race to Amazing 4 Step Discovery:

1. **Understand your strengths as a company, team, or individual.** Think about those things or characteristics that have survived through the years, what your customers first think of as your true attributes. What has defied time and sustained you against your competition? If you're a solo entrepreneur, what are your personal strengths? If you're a large corporation with a plan and accountability, what are your division's, department's, and team's strengths?

Many companies host an annual retreat or strategy session where they do a SWOT analysis. This is a way to get a great discussion around strengths, weaknesses, opportunities, and threats. If you'll recall, I did a SWOT analysis early on in my coaching practice with my first client, and discovered that he was the threat. Although it wasn't a positive discovery, it certainly helped us put forth a path and gave us focus in our coaching program.

You may want to do a SWOT analysis with your team as part of your discovery. A best practice is to pull together a cross-functional group or team and give them adequate time to prepare their thoughts to the following outline:

SWOT Exercise and Definition

Strengths: The strong attributes of your company. What has sustained change and time? What is the competitive edge?

Weaknesses: Those things that are getting in the way of success. Not up to par with the competition, and clearly a competitive disadvantage. Often, weaknesses are more costly in time and resources to fix, but if not fixed, could impede progress.

Opportunities: On the horizon, but needs some resources or attention. Often, they just need commitment and dedication, but could make the difference between winning and losing.

Threats: Serious concerns, which could be harmful, even detrimental, to the overall business. Potentially out of your control.

After you complete your SWOT analysis, you should have a better understanding of your strengths and competitive advantages. You'll likely come up with many ideas of things you can do better or different. You won't be able to attack all of them at once, so our recommendation is to take the top opportunities that will have the greatest impact on the business with the lowest cost, and set the rest aside.

Now, look at your strengths and identify the ones that are truly a competitive edge and not just nice to have. Next, begin creating a sales strategy from a position of strength. Forget all of the wild ideas that don't have any real legs or merit for the moment. Focus on a game plan that is playing *big* from a position of strength.

When I moved to Washington, DC to expand the federal government business, I knew making face-to-face sales calls wasn't my strength, but that was the reason I was there in the Mecca of the federal government. If you recall, I was comfortable behind the phone dialing for dollars. When I first arrived, I spent the first six months on the phone doing just that, rather than fighting the Beltway Bandits and wasting time in traffic. Once I created a solid revenue stream, I hired great people whose strength was face-to-face selling, and they certainly taught me a thing or two. With this approach I gained better results faster, as I was having fun playing from a position of strength. I'm sure the owners didn't mind, since they wanted profitable business results, quickly.

2. **What is happening in your market? What is the competition doing?** Not so you do what they're doing, but determine what you need to do better. It is prudent to do your homework and study the competition. I recommend that you have some of your team members tasked with understanding the top three to four competitors in your market and present it to the group. Often, companies "think" they know what the competition is up to, but it's important to take the time and really study them.

You'll never get ahead of the competition by being reactive to what they're doing. Being proactive is the only way to ensure that you supersede their competitive pressures. This will help you determine what your offensive and your defensive plans should be.

Understand who and what the competition is focused on. How are they approaching the market? What is their messaging? Where are you vulnerable against them? It's time to include how you're going to beat them at their own game in your plan.

3. **Where and how is your current business growing?** Get the facts, gather the trends, and analyze the data intelligence, so your strategy is built from a position of fact and

not opinion. Remember, knowledge is power. Analyze the business year-over-year: compare revenue, margins, product categories, or service offerings by customer, sales rep, or division. Understand the net/net comparison for the business.

We suggest segmenting your market by size, geography, or vertical markets. Understand where your business is growing specifically, and where it's falling off. Are there certain segments, product categories, or salespeople that are more profitable than others? What size or types of customer or customers are more loyal? By answering these questions through data analysis, you'll be able to better determine where you want to put your attention, and what the priorities are for your sales strategy.

Tom, The Sales Leader

 As a sales leader, Tom was very methodical in his approach to his sales strategies at the beginning of each year. It wasn't until they did a deep dive into the data that he discovered some significant trends and areas they needed to pay attention to in the upcoming year.

It was no surprise to Tom that their largest accounts had the highest margins and were the most loyal, but he didn't realize that this group of accounts made up 83 percent of their overall business.

Meanwhile, their small accounts were extremely unprofitable, and the year-over-year retention rate was 57 percent on that category of customer. Yet, there were thousands of accounts that made up this segment. They immediately put in their sales strategy to focus on the "ideal customer" in terms of size and compatibility, and took their attention off of selling to just anyone, especially their smaller account segment. With this group, they decided to raise their minimum orders, change their pricing arrangements, and start charging a shipping fee. If those customers didn't like the new program and decided to go away, well, it was actually okay because net/net they weren't profitable in the first place.

These smaller accounts were very price-focused and had lots of choices in the market. Now, the sales team could spend their time nurturing the larger accounts, continuing to create value, and make them lifelong customers. At the same time, they became the new targeted prospecting list for all the right reasons. Would Tom have come up with the same go-to-market strategy if he hadn't taken the deep dive into the data and trends? I don't think so. Certainly not intentionally.

4. **Who is your ideal customer and target market?** This is the obvious next question in determining what your specific go-to-market strategies are going to be. You can gain this knowledge through step number three, then get more specific on what their needs and circumstances are. What is changing in their world and what are their requirements? Where are they located geographically? Are they financially stable? What are their future needs, and will you be able to continue to exceed their expectations so that they remain loyal? These questions will help you create your power messaging approach to obtain that business. After all, it's all about them, not about you.

Often we ask business owners about their target market or ideal customers. They tend to take a broad brush and want to sell to everyone, and don't want to be particular. They want everyone to be their customer. When I asked questions to better understand a recent client's target market, they said, "They pitch what they sell, and sell what they pitch." That meant to me that they're changing their sales strategy based on reacting to customer's needs, and are willing to compromise their approach for the next big deal. That might not sound so bad, and it's worked for them. Up to this point, they have grown 200 percent year-over-year. But, at some point, they will need to get more systemized and targeted in order to continue having sustainable growth.

When you determine who the "best customer" is, it becomes a lot easier to put an aggressive and more targeted sales and marketing campaign together. All of a sudden, they're responding because they're connecting with your message. You're the expert. There's something to say for getting "rich in your niche." When you're committed to your target market, you'll naturally make better business decisions, and create solutions to meet their needs and attract new business.

As you can see, there is a lot of reflection during the discovery phase, before you can finalize and document your winning strategy. Part of your Race to Amazing is recognizing those times when it's important to take a pause, and begin working on your business. This is where management and leadership intersect the most. It's important to get away from the day-to-day and become more futuristic, as well as having the strategic vision that's needed to move your organization to a new level.

During *Race to Amazing*, you will be identifying what you can do to be more effective in this area. Sales leaders can't lead effectively if they don't have a strategic vision. I am certain, if you use these suggested steps during the Discovery Phase you will build a realistic and successful plan based on sound judgment, and from a position of strength and facts.

Alignment

After you've created your strategic vision, it's critical that your approach meets and aligns with your customer's needs, first and foremost. Alignment is also about aligning your people and your company's strengths to the initiatives, aligning goals to the sales rep activities, aligning marketing and branding to the sales strategy, and aligning compensation plans to motivate the right behavior. Ultimately, alignment is about effectively communicating your company's vision, roles and responsibilities, and making sure that everyone and everything is connected to the big picture.

Terry, The Miscommunicator

 In a recent coaching engagement, I was working with a VP of Sales for a division of a larger corporation. Terry was ultimately responsible for the growth of a product category throughout North America that was valued at $200 million. As he was beginning the New Year planning, we walked through the discovery to build his plan for the year. At one point, he wanted to survey his customers to better understand what their challenges and growth objectives are so that he could better align his products and services. Although surveying these customers resulted in him obtaining a lot of information and gaining insights, he still struggled with getting the buy-in from the corporate headquarters on his strategy for growth.

It was a disheartening moment for both of us when we recognized the misalignment wasn't between him, his team, and the customers. It was between him and his company. The communication of expectations for his department was not clear, therefore holding him, his sales team, and ultimately the entire company back. At this point, he didn't have their support or the buy-in of his boss.

The company wanted Terry to go straight to establishing goals and quotas, but without an agreement on a plan for how to get there. He was stopped in his tracks, feeling defeated, not supported, and slowly losing confidence. After this realization, we worked on the framework of the message and aligned it to the overarching company initiatives. All of a sudden, they recognized its importance. His initiative gained followership and momentum and ultimately a reorganizational structure that eliminated confusion and enabled him to sell and market his products and services more effectively.

Alignment isn't just top-down. Often as a sales leader, you may have to manage the alignment up the food chain and double-check to make sure that it remains aligned throughout. Misalignment can be the biggest culprit to failure.

**On your Race to Amazing, ensure
you've created an alignment of:**

- Ideas that are clear and aligned to the big picture, and well understood.
- Strategy that is written and aligns with the business growth needs.
- Communications that are consistent and align with the mission and vision.
- Teams that are aligned with each other.
- Goals that are aligned to the activities and growth objectives.
- Expectations that are clear and align to individual and company goals.
- Marketing that is aligned to the sales strategy.

. . . .

Discovery and Alignment Checklist

☐ I understand my company's strengths and opportunities against the competition.

☐ I've reviewed the trends in my industry along with my variety of market segments.

☐ I've taken a deep dive into the numbers to better understand where business is being retained and lost.

☐ I have a clear understanding of my ideal customers or "best customers" and their characteristics to better target them.

☐ I understand the value of alignment, the various areas to consider, and the responsibility to ensure proper alignment for strategy success.

CHAPTER 7—GROW YOUR BUSINESS WITH CPR

**"Your most unhappy customers are your
greatest source of learning."**

—Bill Gates

As a sales leader, one of your greatest responsibilities and challenges is to be able to take the big picture and break it down into easy, implementable actions. Creating a go-to-market strategy is the obvious first step. This is your vision and plan based on sound judgment, but it needs to be easily understood by everyone in order to properly execute it and get the results you're seeking.

There isn't a business model for executing a go-to-market strategy that I don't like. However, not all models work for every situation or company. So I'd like to share with you a winning model that has worked for me throughout my career. I've also seen this model work successfully for many of our clients. One of the reasons I think that it works so well is that it's extremely memorable and very easy to implement. I often refer to it as "the meat and potatoes" of sales-strategy creation.

The simple name for this is the CPR Model. You can remember it by the adage of "Breathing life into your business with CPR!" Or, "Save your business with CPR." The C stands for conversion, which involves obtaining brand-new customers. The P stands for penetration. The focus here is on selling more into existing accounts. Finally, the R stands for retention. Here your focus is on creating loyalty among your customers so you effectively hold onto them and keep them coming back for more work with you.

The CPR Model is a balancing act between sales and marketing activities. First, it's important for you to know where your business is currently coming from and where you're losing accounts and/or sales. Begin looking at how much of your business has increased as a result of retaining customers, selling more to existing accounts, and getting brand-new customers. If you have clearly defined actionable plans in all three areas of C, P, and R going on simultaneously, then your business will naturally grow.

For example, if you've focused your sales organization more on managing or retaining existing accounts, your sales pipeline isn't full of new accounts. As a result, you may be in trouble when a large client doesn't renew their contract or goes away.

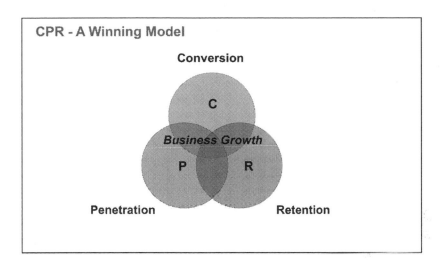

If you're going to use the CPR Model to manage and execute your sales strategies, it's very important that you understand the clear distinctions between the three areas:

1. **Conversion:** Acquiring new business and converting the accounts from your competitors to your company. Conversion strategies are often thought of as your *prospecting plan*. What are you specifically doing to be intentional and aggressive in winning new business? What is your approach and sales process for prospecting for new customers? Are there enough prospects in your sales pipeline at all times?

2. **Penetration:** Selling more to existing accounts by offering current customers additional products and services. Basically, it's selling more of what you have, and ensuring your customers are continuing to grow. Penetrating into accounts isn't just about revenue growth, but overall

profitability growth as well. The one-stop-shop philosophy is quite popular for penetration strategies. It is a lot easier to sell more to existing accounts that already know and love you. The probability of selling to an existing customer is 60 to 70 percent. The probability of selling to a new prospect is 5 to 20 percent—*Marketing Metrics*.

3. **Retention:** Holding onto what you have, not just the number of accounts or customers you currently have but more so the total revenue and profitability that those accounts bring you. Retention is also about ensuring that your customers are loyal and continue to use your products and services at the same level that they always have. Remember, to keep your customers loyal, they need to feel like they can trust you. Even more importantly they will stay and promote your good work to others when you *exceed* their expectations. In a competitive environment, just satisfying them isn't enough to retain them.

In most industries, you would be foolish to think that you could retain more than 90 percent of your clients. Contracts expire, businesses close or downsize, and they may naturally use less of your products or services. Retention is more than just building good relationships, providing great customer service, and doing the day-to-day management of accounts well. It is about constantly developing new ways to keep your customers and always exceeding their expectations.

What is great about the CPR Model is that it can be used in most businesses, regardless of their industry, size, product, or service. The CPR Model can be applied to your local laundromat, beauty salon, or restaurant. It also can be used with small, independent businesses as well as Fortune 500 companies, and some of the biggest high-tech and low-tech companies in the world.

Think about your own company where the CPR Model is already working for you. Do you know your conversion, penetration, and retention rates? Do you have a clearly defined strategy in all three areas to ensure that you have sustainable business growth? If you're a small business owner, what is your CPR strategy? If you're a salesperson or sales manager for a large Fortune 500 company, what is your personal or team CPR plan? Regardless of your business size or type, you can use this model to help you stay in a sales leadership position.

CPR in Action

When I asked myself a defining question I introduced in Chapter 1, "What were you doing when you were ten?" I remembered those early days when my father had his first sales position as an independent Bestline distributor. I'm sure he'd never heard of the CPR Model, but he certainly used its methodology integrating it into the way he managed and grew his business. It was 1970. He sent his eight-year-old child (that would be me) door-to-door selling, dressed in her "Sunday best" purple dress and black patent-leather shoes, to win the hearts and minds of whomever answered the door.

He dropped me off in the rich part of town. I was to demonstrate the Bestline B15 Carpet Shampoo, using a simple wooden clipboard that held a small piece of beige carpet glued to it. I was to draw on the carpet with a bright red crayon, spray the carpet cleaner on the spot and "Ta-da!" the spot miraculously disappeared. That was my first official sales position and his conversion strategy—and it worked.

Then, two weeks later, he would take me back to the same neighborhood introducing a different Bestline product such as Orange Scented Multi-Purpose Air Deodorizer, PH 7 Shampoo, and ZIF All Purpose Cleaner. Clearly, this was his penetration plan to sell more of the product line to those households that enjoyed one of them already. It was also his retention strategy, as these customers looked forward to me stopping by on a regular basis to see what they might need. As you can see, creating a CPR strategy doesn't have to be complicated, and it can have compounding results and impact when you align your marketing strategy to it.

And here is a story to further illuminate how to create a strong conversion strategy. Take the day I was walking home from school and caught my breath in excitement upon seeing a shiny, gold 1970 Cadillac Eldorado in our driveway. I thought for sure someone important was at our house to visit. I quickly ran up the driveway to see who was visiting and saw my father standing by the Cadillac beaming with pride and smiling ear-to-ear. He shouted, "It's ours!" I jumped inside behind the wheel and started playing with the electric windows and asked, "Are we rich dad?" He said, "No, sweetheart, we're not rich, but everyone will think we are." Certainly at that time I didn't quite get it, and didn't learn for years that it was rented.

If you recall, Bestline was somewhat of a pyramid scheme. He needed to get neighbors, friends, and family wanting to represent Bestline so that he could build his team and his business through residual income. If they saw that he was doing so well that we could afford a brand new Cadillac Eldorado, then it must be a good business opportunity. I reflect back on that memory today, and see how this marketing plan aligned to his conversion strategy of getting more people to sell Bestline for him. Brilliant!

As you can see, there is no need to make the CPR Model and strategies complicated. The key to creating the right CPR ideas and plan is to first follow the "go-to-market" strategy methodology in the previous chapter. Once you study your ideal customer's needs, look at your competition and business trends to determine where your revenue and profits are currently coming from. The best way to look at business trends for this analysis is by viewing your past two-rolling customer data timeframes. As a result you'll see your business growth and decreases over a back-to-back period of time to obtain a "true trend."

Some clients like to compare their year-to-date versus prior year-to-date customer data for comparable time frames. Although this analysis can be helpful to understand that set time frame, it's not the best view when you're running a CPR analysis. You may be missing certain months that could affect the trends. We recommend reviewing your current six months versus your prior six months or your current twelve months versus your prior twelve months, for your CPR analysis.

You may even want to take a deeper dive into your data that will allow you to look at the CPR numbers in a variety of ways. For example, perhaps your business segments are large, medium, and small accounts. Or maybe you choose a vertical market segmentation. We recommend to many clients that they look at their overall business CPR rates, but also break their rates down into segments that make sense for them, as well as looking at each sales rep and their individual CPR numbers. For larger organizations, you may want to compare managers, teams, and divisions.

Next Step in CPR Analysis

Separate all of your accounts or customers into one of the three areas as follows:

Conversion Accounts: those accounts that have new revenue in the most current timeframe and should have zero sales in the prior time frame.

Penetration Accounts: These are accounts that grew from the earlier time frame to the current time frame.

Retention Accounts: These are accounts that were down in revenue or profitability and/or completely went away from the prior time frame to the current one.

At this stage, your customers are either falling into a C, P, or R category. Once these accounts are separated in their respective areas, total that section's revenue, and divide it by your total company revenue to get your CPR percentage rates. This will be the percentage of your business that was new, grew, or was lost during those comparable timeframes. Retention rates are calculated by the reciprocal. So, for example, if you lost 20 percent of your business, it would be calculated as an 80 percent retention rate.

Note the following example:

CPR – Formula
Prior Year Revenue – $600,000
Churn 25% – ($150K)
= 75% Retention
= $450K – *base line number*
Penetration 15% = $67,500
Conversion 5% = $22,500
Total Net Growth = -10% ($60K) =
$540,000 projected for next year

There are a lot of businesses that may not have the customer data and information to analyze in order to determine what the CPR rates are. The whole purpose of the analysis is to help you understand what areas need the most focus and attention in your organization in order to grow your overall business. From this knowledge you can create specific, actionable plans in those specific C, P, and R areas that align with your overarching business growth strategy.

It's ideal to create your CPR strategies during your business planning. As a result you can then be very intentional and proactive in executing them, knowing they align to your big picture, and are built based on sound judgment and facts. There will be times when everything is seemingly going great, even though you may or may not have a real business plan for growth. But then something suddenly surprises you and hits you hard or there might be a significant shift in your business that may be beyond your control, and now you need to respond. This would be a case for an emergency CPR requiring you to breathe life back into your business quickly.

Freddie's Inn

Unfortunately, the Bestline Company shut down and my father was stuck with a bruised ego and a basement full of soap. But he always had a taste for entrepreneurship, and now because of his Bestline experience, something deep in his soul started bubbling up creating a reemergence of new hope and new possibilities. He had developed a sustainable winning attitude.

So in 1974, he purchased a small tavern in Mine 37, a coal mining town a few miles west of Windber, Pennsylvania. Like many of the other coal mines in the area, they were numbered, that is, Mine 30, Mine 32, Mine 40, and all looked very similar. There would be rowhouses, a company store, and a small tavern where residents in the area could gather to enjoy a nice meal or a drink with friends.

This was a turning point in my family's life as we moved just a few miles from my hometown to live above the tavern, Freddie's Inn, which we now owned. For me, it meant a new school district, a change in high school, and the anxiety of making new friends. It also meant that my three brothers and I were instantly put to work.

We were a big part of our family-owned business, learning at an early age about the importance of a strong work ethic and the deep and rich value of great customer service. When we turned thirteen, my siblings and I worked in the kitchen making pizzas and flipping hamburgers. At sixteen, we waited on tables, and on our eighteenth birthdays, we weren't permitted to go out with friends, because we were then old enough to bartend.

In the early years, the coal miners would come to the tavern in the morning, after their night shift, for a shot and a beer. Fortunately, when we bought Freddie's Inn, it already had a great reputation for its fresh, homemade pizza, wings dings, and a fun, local crowd. Many of the regulars lived within walking distance, which made it very convenient to visit Freddie's at least several times a week. And when it came to new customers (conversions), you could always count on my father enthusiastically greeting them with a warm slap on the back or hug and giving them their first "drink on the house," making them feel instantly welcome. We always had "a good crowd," as my father would put it.

But as with any business, you can't take success for granted. If you want to continue to grow and prosper, you need to be able to adapt quickly to changes and consistently have a plan for growth.

About a year and a half after we bought Freddie's, I remember business slowing down more than normal, and our family working more hours because we couldn't afford to hire outside help. But even more disconcerting was that my father seemed worried about paying bills, and I could see this on his face and in his actions. This wasn't his natural behavior to have a negative attitude or seemingly depressed, so I knew that something was seriously wrong.

Then one morning as I was running to the front door to catch the school bus, I noticed my father in a dark corner booth with his hand on his head. I went over to him and asked what was wrong. He said to me, with tears in his eyes, "The coal mine is shutting down. We may need to sell Freddie's." It seemed as though we had just moved in and all was going great, and then with a flip of a switch, everything was changing.

At that moment, all I wanted to do was hug my father to cheer him up and offer encouraging words to give him hope—the type of hope and inspiration that he gave naturally to so many people. I reminded him of how successful he was with Bestline, how he started that business from scratch, and how he grew it through existing customers. The next thing I knew, we were dreaming out loud, talking about all the possibilities for Freddie's Inn. He turned over the paper placemat that was sitting on the booth tabletop and divided the placemat into three sections with vertical lines, and, right then and there, we started planning.

We asked, "What we could do to get brand new customers to drive to Freddie's in Mine 37 for dinner? How could we make sure that when customers came they spent more money? Also what could we do to make sure that current customers would tell their friends and family about Freddie's and continue to come back?" We did not have a name for our planning in those days, but in hindsight, we were building a CPR strategy.

CPR Results

All of a sudden, Freddie's Inn had jazz music in the dining room, and every Friday night there was a different genre of music; bluegrass, rock 'n roll, or country. We began attracting new customers from all over the metropolitan area and they started to spread the word of the great food and fun atmosphere. We started delivering pizza to the local college (University of Pittsburgh at Johnstown) way before Domino's was ever born.

Over the next two years, my father and his friends built Sir Richard's Room (named after my father), which was a large reception hall, adjacent to Freddie's. I remember being in awe of them hauling in the original barn beams from my grandfather's barn. The reception hall could accommodate up to three hundred people, had a stage for live bands, a beautiful twenty-foot stone fireplace, and a running rustic water wheel. It was, by far, the most popular place in the area for wedding receptions and live entertainment, and it offered the best pizza around, with over 350 pizzas sold on a Saturday night. Now that was a good crowd.

I smile when I remember that business plan for Sir Richard's Room; it was intended for penetration, and a back of the napkin drawing, similar to the placemat CPR. Our family worked long hours, but it was a fun atmosphere and a great way to grow up.

Not all emergency CPR strategies will have a happy ending, like Freddie's Inn. The only way CPR strategies can be successful is if they're well planned and properly executed.

Fast forward thirty years, as I look back on my business career, I remember creating and executing sales growth plans using this model. Whether it was my first telesales position selling to the government, opening new office locations, or working as a sales manager for Boise Cascade Office Products, CPR worked. It wasn't until I was a vice president of sales for Corporate Express that I was introduced to the actual term CPR from a consulting firm that was helping us with a large merger. That was when the light bulb went on and I realized that what I had been doing for twenty years had a name.

• •

CPR Exercise

What is your CPR Strategy?

Run a CPR Analysis to determine what percent of your business falls into the three categories.

1. New Accounts – Conversion _____%

2. Selling More, Accounts that Grew – Penetration _____%

3. Maintaining Existing Accounts – Retention _____%

What should the rates be?

C _____%
P _____%
R _____%

What area are you excelling in?

What needs more attention?

Do you have accountability and measurements and monitoring in place, to ensure execution of the plan?

CHAPTER 8—TAKING THE LEAD

"In the end, all business operations can be reduced to
three words: people, product, and profits. Unless you've got
a good team, you can't do much with the other two."

—Lee Iacocca

What exactly is a sales management system? Consider a sales management system as a combination of your personal style of leadership, along with the processes and systems by which you lead and manage others. Amazing things will happen when you create and put this predictable, workable system and style in place.

Sales Management System

 I once received a voice message from one of my clients who was working diligently on his personal sales management system. He was a highly successful salesperson for an $80 million company, and was asked to be a "selling manager" and begin managing a sales team. This common mistake is something we see frequently. Just because someone is a successful sales rep doesn't make them qualified or guaranteed that they will be a successful sales manager. These are two different skill sets. To compound the situation, he was asked to manage a team of people who were previously his peers, and he would be, in essence, competing against them. After a four-month coaching engagement, targeted on sales leadership style and system, I received this memorable voice message: *"Hey Krista, I was driving into work this morning and I just had to send you a message… I'm at peace, organized, enjoying what I'm doing, not stressed, and having fun."* Obviously I loved hearing that! Don't you wish we all could say that? More importantly, it was a testament to what a successful sales management system can do for you.

If you're a sales leader, regardless of the size of your company, and you don't feel this way—it's time to roll up your sleeves. If you're a business owner and you don't believe that your sales manager is successfully leading and executing your vision, then began assessing what they could be doing better or different. It's time to build your sales management system.

Document and Communicate Your Sales Strategies

 Once I started my own coaching and consulting firm, I quickly realized that my clients not only needed help creating their CPR strategies, but also needed a plan for communicating and executing them. We recommend using our DOGOM format. This enables you to take strategy "ideas" and turn them into a documented plan that is easy to understand and to share with others. Think of the DOGOM as the "How to do" behind the "What to do." The five components of a DOGOM are – Description, Objectives, Goal, Owner, Measurement & Monitoring. The format below will better describe the different components of the DOGOM document.

• •

DOGOM Preparation

Below describes the DOGOM acronym:

Description. This is the idea or the "what to do." It should be one or two paragraphs that describe your strategy. It doesn't need to include your objectives or goals, as they will be outlined separately below. It should be clear, concise, and easy to understand by anyone outside of your company or industry.

Objectives. These should be bulleted items of what you want to achieve and why. What specifically are your intentions, reasons, and expectations for executing your strategy?

Goals. Goals should be specific statements that are measurable, realistic, and attainable. They should have a "target" number associated with them, and a specific timeline for completion.

Owner. This is the one person who is ultimately responsible for the success of the strategy. Owners should be intimately involved in leading their teams and holding others accountable to meeting their objectives and goals. In most cases, this is the role of the sales leader or the business owner.

Measurement/Monitoring. This is the most important and often forgotten component of the DOGOM strategy creation. How will you measure and monitor the activities and goals for this strategy? How will you hold others accountable? It can be tied to reports and metrics, but should contain rewards and recognition for accomplishments. Often this includes regular meetings, sales contests, and weekly, monthly, or quarterly check-ins. How you measure and monitor should be predictable, clear, and consistent.

• •

At K.Coaching, we learned that once companies adopted the DOGOM format for documenting strategies, they began using it in other departments within the organization. It isn't uncommon to have three or four documented DOGOMs aligned to your CPR strategy ideas. Once you have them, it's time to prioritize. We suggest reviewing all of them at the same time, then ask yourself,

"Which one is going to be the easiest to implement with the lowest cost, and will also have the greatest impact on our success?" In other words, "Which one is going to make the most money?"

As a young sales manager, I felt completely overwhelmed with so many things to do and I had a hard time prioritizing. I recall asking my boss, "How do I prioritize? I have so much on my plate." He said, "Make a list of all of the things that you need to do and then ask yourself 'Which one will make you the most money?' That's the priority." In business, I would agree with him, and it's a great way to determine which DOGOM you need to implement first.

Once you start using the DOGOM format, you'll begin to see momentum behind your strategy ideas. Ideas are just that—ideas. There are thought leaders in all organizations; they just might not be called that. We need thought leaders to create these awesome ideas, and to have the strategic vision, but we also need action leaders that are amazing sales leaders. These are the leaders that can take the idea and make it happen. These are the leaders that can take the vision and relentlessly drive it to completion, through their own actions and the actions of others.

Goals, Objectives, and Tactics

Most businesses will talk about the importance of setting goals and having business objectives, yet rarely do we see them creating the framework or sticking with it. Many managers might perceive setting goals and having a system of accountability as a form of micromanagement. They're reluctant to work through the level of detail required to establish individual activities, milestones, and timelines.

Without an established and clearly understood platform of goals, objectives, and tactics, your sales team is operating without a roadmap or a destination. And without parameters of performance, you can't reasonably reward sales reps for what they accomplish or hold them accountable for what they don't accomplish. It's that simple.

Let's imagine that your Saturday morning golf buddies call you Friday night and say, "Hey, for tomorrow's golf match, we're not going to keep score." What's your incentive to go out and play then? What's your competitive motivation? Without established objectives, your sales team's daily work isn't much different than your non-competitive foursome. They have no clear direction of what to do, no specific tactics on how to do it, and no objective measurement to gauge their performance.

Without clearly defined goals, objectives, and tactics for yourself and your sales organization, you risk perpetuating a culture where the lack of motivation, accountability, and direction leads to complacency. With that kind of environment, how will you achieve the business results you're looking for?

Creating clearly defined goals and objectives for individuals becomes much easier once you've established your DOGOM. Then the employees will understand that their day-to-day activities contribute to the company's overall vision and success. They'll be motivated to achieve more when they can see their contributions are aligned, especially, if they're recognized for their performance and over-achievement.

So, how do you get from recognizing the vital, strategic need for goals, objectives, and tactics to actually creating this structure for your sales organization? As I look back to my first year in sales, we knew specifically what the company's goals were for growth. The specific product targets and our individual activity goals were aligned to the overall company sales plan. This kept everyone focused on selling each day, and we were held accountable to daily activities that rolled up into our monthly, quarterly, and annual goals. We were laser-focused and held accountable daily, but it was a fun, friendly, competitive atmosphere. I remember like it was yesterday. I needed to make twenty phone calls a day, talk to seventeen people, bid on $10,000 a day, and write up at least $5,000 a day in business in order to hit my annual goal of $3 million.

At the end of each day, we were required to write the total dollar amount we bid and how much we sold on a small piece of paper, fold it up, and put it in a wicker basket outside the president's office. Creating, aligning, and communicating sales strategies, individual goals, and accountability doesn't have to be difficult. Management is about planning, organizing, staffing, directing, and measuring. These tasks might involve creating internal processes, written plans, quota setting, measuring and monitoring performance, giving feedback, and holding people accountable. If you are a manager, reread the paragraph, and highlight what you need to work on to improve your management system and style to get better results.

I've asked many business owners to describe their sales management system and I often hear, "We don't have one," or, "We're a small business, and don't really need one." What many fail to realize is how much more efficient they will be if they would take the time to define one. After taking a deeper dive, I usually discovered they do have a system; it just may be missing a few pieces or steps.

Remember, a sales management system creates a predictable process by which you can better manage your sales force, keeping them focused on the proper activities for reaching their goals that are aligned with the company's sales strategy. Worse is when you have these systems and processes in place, but are still not achieving your goals. If that's the case, it's time to look at the people.

Achievement vs. Development

Achievement and development go hand in hand, and often the challenge is creating a balance between them. When a sales leader is so focused on achievement, hitting quotas and exceeding goals, the sales rep will begin to think that that's all that you care about and you don't understand or care about them as individuals. When sales goals aren't achieved, typically sales managers look at their people as failing, but do not look at themselves and what they could have done to improve their system or help develop others to be more successful.

Part of your management system should include a developmental plan for each individual. You're responsible for developing their skills, aligning their activities to their strengths, as well as inspiring and motivating them every step of the way. Achievement on the other hand, is more about hitting the numbers and achieving specific goals and quotas. Very rarely do I see the development area override the achievement, even in a first year or newer sales rep. Let's explore the differences, and determine if you have the balance that your organization needs.

Achievement (Quantity)

The financial goals or commitments that you have to your position in the organization (that is, revenue, margin dollars, profitability). These numbers should be unique and specific to the individual, aligned with realistic expectations based on the territory, experience, and business knowledge. If you have a growth goal that is the same for all your reps, or expect the same type and amount of activity from everyone, it's likely that you're constantly disappointed in the level of achievement from certain people.

Sometimes it's just easier to create corporate-wide benchmarks: everyone needs to grow X percent, everyone needs to bring in X new accounts each month, or everyone needs to sell X million dollars a year. A more targeted strategy, however, involves reconsidering the individual and creating an achievement plan that yields success for both you and your sales rep.

Development (Quality)

The core competencies of the sales reps, their business knowledge and experience, prospecting skills, penetration focus, and account management abilities; the professional quality of their work, attitude, willingness, follow-through and teamwork. Managers often overlook this area. Sales reps may not be achieving their goals and objectives, but are also not receiving the kind of guidance, training, and development necessary to help them identify weaknesses and sharpen their effectiveness. I often see employee development in an organization, if it exists at all, applied with a broad brush: reps receive generalized training classes with no company-specific context or individual attention.

Successful sales managers get to know their sales reps and align training or development specifically to the reps' needs and company strategies. For development, you should have a list of core competencies that successful sales reps must possess in order to succeed, and score your reps on a scale that you can share with them.

Use this information to create a personal development plan in partnership with your sales rep for both of you to work on throughout the year. The developmental plan includes monthly and annual reviews, measuring the success of an individual's career path and skill development.

It doesn't matter whether you have one salesperson or multiple teams and hundreds of people. Identifying individual achievement goals and continuously working on individual developmental areas are key elements of your sales management system, and your overall team's success.

If you've been following our step-by-step guide to building your sales management system, you can see the need for employees to come to work with a clear idea of company expectations, an understanding of their individual roles in the overall company success, and a belief in the company's conviction in investing the time and resources into their professional development.

Additional Best Practices

- Regularly scheduled sales team meetings focused on strategies, team success, and meeting company-wide objectives.
- Regularly scheduled one-on-one meetings to privately

discuss their achievement and developmental plans and status.

- Provide regular and timely feedback in-between meetings.
- Conduct a more formal annual review.

Once you've incorporated these elements into your management system, you'll naturally be building a culture of accountability, ultimately providing your sales team with a roadmap to success.

At K.Coaching, we administer a sales management system and style assessment. Below is a shorter version of the complete assessment that you can find on www.racetoamazing.com. The results will enable you to create your own plan and path for moving forward to becoming an amazing leader. Take your time and answer these questions thoughtfully and honestly.

• •

 Are You a Coach, a Nice Guy, or MIA?

1. Do you have a clearly defined sales strategy?

Yes (3)
Kind of (2)
No (1)

2. Do you clearly define sales rep goals and activities?

Yes (3)
Not really (2)
No (1)

3. Do you meet one-on-one with your direct reports for coaching, mentoring on their personal and business development?

Yes, consistently (3)
Sometimes; I'm thinking about doing it more (2)
No (1)

4. Do you have a written business plan to achieve your own goals?

Yes (3)
I don't, but I have a plan in my head. (2)
No (1)

5. Do you have quotas and a method for measuring and monitoring sales rep performance?

Yes (3)
No (1)

6. Do you communicate performance and sales results to everyone on a regular and consistent basis?

Yes (3)
No (1)

7. Do you have an organized and predictable sales management system?

Yes (3)
No (1)

Total score_____

7–12   MIA
13–17 Nice Guy
18–21 Coach

*85 percent of those surveyed score within the "nice guy" category.

• •

While on the surface there certainly doesn't seem anything wrong with being a "nice guy," in management terms, it limits your ability to get sustainable business results. Your sales reps most likely consider you a friend, rather than a leader. In the nice guy environment, sales reps typically don't have quotas, clearly defined sales objectives, and aren't likely to be held accountable. They tend to be comfortable, maintain only the status quo, and are unconcerned about their job security. Nice guys often avoid crucial conversations or conflict and therefore avoid offering constructive feedback or performance appraisal; as a result, the individual sales rep finds neither direction nor motivation to develop their full potential.

So how can you progress from a nice guy to a coach? Many of K.Coaching's clients have found themselves in this same situation and have obtained significant business results from our programs for creating a predictable management system and a coaching style of leadership.

Just like in sports, it all starts with a clear vision of what great looks like and what the future holds. After you define and communicate the necessary strategies, then it takes a team to collaborate and work together toward the desired results. They know their position and how their individual and team performance will be aligned and measured. The coach and the team member know the areas that they need to continue to develop to be the best that they can be. The successful coach's style is inspiring, consistent, and predictable to create a team of champions.

All of this may appear overwhelming at first, but any movement you make in the direction of constructing a growth framework will improve business results. Take things one step at a time. You don't want to create a culture shock in your organization, but you do want to establish a renewed atmosphere of motivation and commitment, and a shift toward a performance-based environment.

As you strive to win your Race to Amazing, it's important to pause and reflect on your current sales management system and determine the areas where you can enhance your effectiveness and get better results through others. Start now by making some changes that could elevate you to an inspirational leader and coach.

• •

Sales Management System Checklist

☐ Clearly define and communicate the "Go-to-Market" sales strategy in terms of the company's mission and vision—the "How we are going to get there."

☐ Create the individual goals, objectives, and tactics in terms of the specific achievements to which each individual will be held accountable, that rolls up to the company goals.

☐ Create a development plan for each rep and agree on the training and developmental areas required for an individual to achieve greatest success.

☐ Create a weekly meeting that keeps the sales reps focused on the company strategy; reward and recognize achievement.

☐ Have a monthly one-on-one meeting with each individual rep, reviewing their achievements, and determine what you can do to help them develop additional skills in the areas that matter to get better results.

☐ Observe, coach, and provide both positive and constructive feedback to keep them on track.

☐ Reward, recognize, and celebrate the success.

CHAPTER 9—LEADERSHIP WITH A COACH APPROACH

"One common thought managers have is that
they will lose their power if they take on a coaching role.
What they don't realize is that they end up with more
power by being a coach rather than a manager."

—Byron and Catherine Pulsifer

When you think of coaches, you likely think of successful leaders from the world of sports: Vince Lombardi, Tom Landry, Billy Martin, or Tommy Lasorda. What do these and other successful coaches have in common?

They're certainly leaders in their field; each had an ability to guide individuals of varying and differing talents to work together and succeed as a team. Each knew how to align team objectives and goals and communicate these ideas effectively. Each knew how to make his players understand their responsibilities, and how to motivate and inspire each of them to be the best that they could be.

One of my favorite quotes on coaching comes from legendary Dallas Cowboys head coach, Tom Landry, who so eloquently said, "A coach is…someone who tells you what you don't want to hear, who has you see what you don't want to see, so you can be who you've always known you can be."

Business Coaching

Given the importance of coaching to success, you can understand why business coaching has emerged as an effective method for motivating and challenging already successful leaders to attain an even higher level of achievement. Many companies are engaging professional business coaches to further develop their leaders and high performers. Business coaching is considered a benefit, perk, and investment in the areas of personal development and leadership skills for a company's high potential employees.

At K.Coaching, we work with already successful leaders who want to become even more amazing, and get to the next level of personal and professional achievement. Having a coaching style of leadership will get them there that much faster. Many businesses have changed their style of leadership and management to more of a coaching approach to develop and train their employees and future leaders. Statistics show that training in conjunction with coaching increases retention and productivity by 83 percent!

How can you be a coach in your own business? Many companies

today are teaching their leaders to develop a coaching style. To begin this transformation, an organization's management processes and style need to be defined and predictable, and sales reps need to clearly understand their leaders' expectations and their own accountability to the process. This is often the foundational difference between the nice guy in the previous chapter, and a coaching style of leadership. As you read through what a coach can do for business, equate that to what a coach might do similarly with a sports team.

A Coach...

- Aligns sales activities to the company's vision and sales strategy.
- Creates goals and continuously develops the team.
- Holds the reps accountable.
- Listens, understands, and has an emotional connection to the team.
- Motivates and inspires to get the best out of others.

The ultimate objective of leading with a coaching style is to achieve the desired results through others. Just as with sports, the coach cannot perform for players on the field; rather, the coach must teach, guide, inspire, and motivate players to work in concert to achieve the team's goals.

A coach in a business environment achieves this by listening to team members and working closely with each of them as individuals. I often say it's important to understand an individual's obstacles with your head, heart, and gut—*not* just business results.

Get to Know Your Team

Establish an emotional connection by understanding what motivates each member personally and professionally. I recommend a "reflections" questionnaire to many of my clients. The reflections questionnaire offers a valuable first step to developing relationships and embarking on a coaching style. The reflections questionnaire allows for an open discussion where you, as a coach, can listen and understand what is important to your sales reps and what motivates them. You can also understand areas of challenge to help you be a better coach and guide your employee toward greater success.

Below is a sample reflections questionnaire that can help you begin to develop a coaching style of management of sales—these can be modified for other positions. Give it to your team members before meeting with them. This gives them time to provide meaningful answers. You'll also need to trade-in your manager/boss hat for a coach's hat. Don't forget: this is your team's meeting. Be a good listener and ask open-ended follow-up questions.

Reflection Questions for Sales

Please answer these questions as clearly and thoughtfully as possible. These questions are designed to stimulate your self-discovery and to make our working relationship together more productive. Feel free to use "bullets" and incomplete sentences.

How are you feeling about working for our company, as part of your career development?

What do you expect from me in my role as your manager?

What can I expect from you in this working relationship?

What challenges do you see facing you with your position?

In what area(s) would you like some coaching and development as it relates to your role?

What gets your blood pumping and makes you excited or motivated?

What is missing from your work life that you could add to make it more complete?

What adjectives describe who you are now, at your core? What adjectives describe who you want to be in the future?

What would you like to see different from me as your manager, to be more effective?

. . . .

If you use the above reflections questionnaire, it will get you in a position where you're thoughtfully listening and understanding them more personally and professionally.

Coaching and Understanding

It's important to realize that employees' wants and needs will be reflected in their behavior or how they act. However, you need to truly understand what is directing their actions. What are the specific goals your team members want to achieve? Understand why these goals are so important to them by exploring what needs of theirs it satisfies. This will help you understand *why* they do what they do, ultimately resulting in a better understanding of each person you coach and their circumstances.

Continue to practice coaching through understanding by being conscientious to create a comfortable environment whereby you have open dialogue and improved two-way communication. The first step is to get in the habit of asking questions rather than telling others what to do.

There is a general misconception of the term *coaching style* of leadership within some organizations. I've heard leaders tell me, "Oh, I coached them on that." What they meant was, they told them what to do or they pointed out what they were doing wrong and corrected them. This isn't coaching. The best way I can express this for you to remember, is that coaching isn't telling, it's understanding.

A Coach Approach

A great example of this is when someone comes into your office to ask you a question and is looking for direction or an answer. Don't just give them the answer. Instead, pause and ask them a question to get them thinking, but also to help you better understand why they have that question in the first place, for example: "What do you think the top three options are?" or "Tell me what you think you should do?"

This approach will also help you better understand the essence of the question or problem. When you begin incorporating understanding into your style, you'll soon discover that when the idea or solution is theirs, they will own it, learn from it, develop, and grow from it.

Outside of the reflections questions or someone coming up with the answers on their own, you can start practicing by making sure that you're asking open-ended questions to get the dialogue going.

This requires that you begin to be more sincere, inquisitive, and present during conversations you're having. For example, if you ask, "How is that new account coming along?" You might get a one or two word answer such as, "Great," or, "Pretty good." If you were to ask, "Is the new account closed?" you would likely get a yes or no answer.

Open-ended questions encourage the sharing of ideas and information. For instance, "Describe to me what you discovered was most important to the customer?" You can also use open-ended questions to explore alternatives and possibilities, "What are some other things you can do?" Begin using words such as "Tell me about," "Describe to me," or "Give me some examples." This will get the ball rolling on more clearly understanding the circumstance and the person, enabling you to be a better coach.

The concept of asking questions will not only enhance the level of dialogue, but also empower you to listen better and further understand their level of understanding on a particular subject. Now, you'll no longer be making assumptions and can truly further develop and coach them in the right areas.

Coaching and Listening

Listening is an acquired skill and can be very difficult for busy leaders who are on-the-go to learn and become proficient at it. When you conduct these reflection meetings and have other coaching conversations, use good listening skills. Remember, your goal is to truly understand and connect emotionally to your team member.

Here are some pointers for becoming a more effective listener and creating an open and safe environment:

Avoid distractions. Put your other work aside, face the person who is talking, and focus your attention on them. There is nothing worse than you responding to an email or checking your phone when someone else is talking to you and you say to them, "I'm listening." You're not truly listening. Statistics show that only 2 percent of people can multitask effectively. Focusing on more than one thing decreases your productivity by 40 percent, so turn away from your computer, or put down your phone, and just listen.

One habit that has worked for me is when I have a pre-scheduled coaching conversation over the phone, in order to truly avoid distractions, I physically move myself away from my computer and into my big blue chair, aka my coaching chair.

Make eye contact and smile. A smile shows interest and helps put the other person at ease. When you look someone in the eye, they will sense an immediate connection.

Don't interrupt. Wait for them to finish and give your full attention until it's your turn to speak. This is a hard one for some people who are quick to talk over others or move the conversation along quickly because they have the answers. But interrupting isn't just not listening, it's inconsiderate and rude.

Relax. Use relaxed, yet attentive body language. If you seem agitated or stressed the other person might sense that as distracted, uninterested, or rushed.

Use casual language. Use short expressions such as "I see," and, "Yes, tell me more," to communicate that you're following what's being said.

Be friendly. Create a comfortable atmosphere that encourages openness. Often tone can be misinterpreted, so be careful of how others might hear your expressions. When you're under pressure or stressed, your tone may change without you recognizing it. Others may not know how you're feeling and may assume that you're personally agitated with them because they're being bothersome.

Paraphrase what's said. Say it back to the other person, reiterating what you've just heard, but in your own words. A good way to say this is "If I heard you correctly..." or, "If I understand what you're saying, you're feeling..."

Coaching and Observing

In addition to understanding and listening, careful observation is an essential coaching skill. Observation can be difficult if you're not working alongside your associates or have a remote management situation. However, it's a powerful tool to incorporate into your coaching style. Imagine a football coach, coaching his team through virtual meetings!

Begin by creating an environment where you can observe the work and interactions of your team as often as possible. It is human nature to listen to others' opinions or make judgment calls. A coaching style of leadership recognizes the importance and value of observing others and forming your own opinions based on facts rather than perceptions.

As you gather insights, you'll start to analyze the data and take the time to form theories about what's happening. As you think about an issue, it's great to be able to bounce your observations off of others, and test your theories.

No matter what the coaching situation, always start with careful observation. Maybe you want to assess if someone is ready for a new position or responsibilities? Perhaps you need to analyze a problem performer, and watch their behavior and actions? Or you may want to find chances for positive feedback and recognition.

As you develop your observation skills, keep in mind the following guidelines:

Address the Impact of the Behavior

When you observe an individual's behavior, ask yourself exactly what the person is doing or not doing effectively. Your answer should address the impact of their behavior on goals and coworkers, rather than internalizing or making it personal. What impact does the person's actions have on achieving your group's goals or objectives? What impact does it have on other people? Remember, be careful to separate observations from judgments or assumptions.

Curbside Coaching

For sales leaders, one of the best opportunities for demonstrating a coach approach to leadership is by spending one-on-one time observing, listening, and coaching salespeople. There is no better time or place than working side-by-side with them, and having those conversations right after you've observed certain behaviors.

Are you taking time to engage in field coaching with each new salesperson and existing experienced ones? Make sure you don't neglect this crucial step in sales development and you have a coaching style of leadership.

For example, you've hired a superstar and the classroom training for your new salesperson is finished. Is their training really complete? Not a chance! Field coaching is the next step and the most important part of a well-rounded and world-class sales training system. You can modify the outline below when observing, but also make this process a standard part of your sales training for every new hire at your company.

Planning Your Coaching Day

1. Tell your new salesperson the exact day and time you'll be working with them.

2. Ask them to prepare a schedule of activities planned for the

day, including prospect appointments, any client customer care, and follow-up contacts with prospects from the previous week or month.

3. Discuss how each new prospect appointment will be handled and have your salesperson take you through their "perfect" presentation or a "mock" prospect telephone call.

4. Have your new salesperson use their CRM or practice completing all the necessary paperwork required by your company for prospect follow-up.

Start your coaching day by explaining to your new salesperson that you're there to assist them in becoming more successful, and your time together will be a positive and productive experience. Ask them to first watch your "perfect" presentation and your telephone demonstration. This will make them more comfortable working with you, and they will aspire to model your world-class skills.

Handling Your Coaching Day

Ask your salesperson to introduce you so each prospect knows who you are. This should be done with little fanfare, and it's optional to share your job title. Let your new salesperson handle the entire appointment with each prospect, as the purpose of your coaching day is to observe them in action. If necessary, tell your new salesperson that you'll be happy to help them during any prospect presentation, but only if they turn to you and ask you for specific feedback. Otherwise, it's your role to observe them and take detailed notes for review after the presentation and appointment are complete.

Powerful managerial coaching is like learning to ride a bicycle. At first you were scared, then you rode your bicycle with training wheels, then the training wheels came off and you zigzagged and wobbled around, and finally, you could ride your bicycle all by yourself. Your new salesperson is experiencing the same emotions and just needs your kindness and support while learning the skills you expect.

Great coaching means listening three times as much as you speak. If coached properly, your new salesperson will soon be "riding their new bike," having great fun, and generating profitable results.

Recapping Your Coaching Day

After each appointment is completed, spend the next ten to fifteen minutes recapping each presentation meeting. Ask your new salesperson to describe for you exactly what went "perfect" and compliment them on their progress. Then, ask them to tell you exactly what they would "improve" for their next presentation. Help them find ways to improve each presentation and watch to see their progress as your day with them continues.

At the end of the day, ask your salesperson to watch you give one more "perfect" presentation and another telephone demonstration and ask for their critique. This will serve as a powerful model for them to remember, long after this day is complete.

After you invest time field coaching a new salesperson, take fifteen to twenty minutes the very next day to draft a letter thanking them for your time together. In the letter, praise them for progress made and recap the areas you would like them to develop and/or improve. Place this letter in your salesperson's file and make a note in your appointment book to review it again in thirty and sixty days. Remember: quick follow-up and reinforcement for every new salesperson during the first sixty days is most important.

Motivation

One of my favorite quotes on motivation is from Zig Ziglar. *"People often say that motivation doesn't last. Well, neither does bathing — that's why we recommend it daily."*

A coach approach to leadership is a method for getting the results that you were looking for, through others. Wouldn't it be great if every sales rep who worked for you was motivated only by money? They would then feel their own incentive to make the most of each sales day. They would be opening up new accounts, going after larger deals, manage their margins without being asked, and focused on growing their territory year over year, regardless of the economy… just so they can make more money.

I think we can all agree that it's not that simple, or likely. I talk with many entrepreneurs and sales leaders, and this is a hot topic. They're seeing their sales reps more frustrated than ever with competitive environments. Reps are having difficulty adjusting to changes in their methods for going to market and establishing relationships. They're confused about expectations. As a result, they're not finding the same success they did in the past. In addition, many companies are seeing complacency settling in; their more tenured reps are seemingly happy with their current salaries and standards of living, and don't feel any incentive to work any harder than they need to sustain that.

What do you do? How can you change their attitude? Can you motivate and manage them to higher achievements? Many people don't think they can affect these changes, believing that motivation comes from within. But some of you do know that you can impact the results in a positive way, but you're just not sure how. We can all agree, however, that it's certainly worth a try.

Let's explore that nature of motivation and how you can influence and affect the actions of others. This is the ultimate skill for a business or sports coach. Yes, motivation comes from within, but as employers and managers, your influence can make a difference on the actions of others in a motivating or a demotivating way.

Motivation is a set of attitudes that direct behavior. It's the "what," "why," and "how" behind the reasons for our actions. First and foremost, we need to understand why our employees do what they do; what is driving their behavior? And how can you coach them so they're motivated and get the results you're looking for and they desire?

Another one of my favorite quotes on motivation is from Dwight Eisenhower: *"Motivation is the art of getting people to do what you want them to do because they want to do it."* The key words for me are "art" and "because they *want* to do it." Yes, motivation is an art and a science. It's our job to figure out what drives people's thinking, attitudes, and behaviors so we can influence and impact them in a positive way, until ultimately the results we want become the results they want.

The Art and Science of Motivation

You may be familiar with Maslow's hierarchy of needs and his theory of human motivation. This model is certainly worth reviewing to understand that people are motivated by achieving basic needs and when those basic needs are present and felt, people are positively affected and their actions show it. These basic needs can be considered hot buttons or triggers to which individuals respond positively in their environment. They naturally build upon each other in a hierarchy, ultimately reaching personal fulfillment and growth.

If you overlay this model with what you know about an individual's thoughts and desires, you can clearly influence their behavior in a positive way. And this is where the science of motivation meets the art.

Let's look at this model from a business perspective and determine if you have a work environment that can aid in fulfilling the basic human psychological needs that create motivation, or if, conversely, your environment or circumstances might dampen your employees' motivations:

- **Biological and physiological needs:** Basic life needs such as air, food, water, shelter, sleep, and money.
- **Security**: Secure environment, stability, and non-threatening circumstances.
- **Belonging and love needs:** Sense of being a part of something larger than oneself, a team; fair treatment; fulfilling social, family, and professional relationships.
- **Self-esteem:** Confidence, a sense of value as an employee; recognition, prestige, empowerment, achievement, status, and responsibility.

- **Self-actualization:** Personal growth and fulfillment; this is the final level of psychological development that can be achieved when all physical, psychological, and intellectual needs are fulfilled and the "actualization" of full personal potential takes place. This is also the "full realization of one's potential," and at this level, there is high motivation.

Statistics show that the more companies meet the basic needs of their employees, the more motivated their employees will be. Consider how a work environment or a management style that is threatening or one in which employees feel they're not treated fairly, appreciated, or valued, can impact morale.

It's important to identify the factors inhibiting motivation that can be corrected, as well as determining demotivating factors that may be beyond your control. Identify any potentially demotivating circumstances both inside and outside your employees' work environment. In order to figure out what motivates others and how you can influence them, you want to identify any potentially negative circumstances, and determine if you're able to remove any of these barriers or distractions. Try to understand the factors that may be contributing to low levels of motivation, and if they're within your control to change.

Demotivation

Knowing about demotivating circumstances and their implications is a great first step in addressing motivational issues.

- **Low morale:** Are there individuals in your company

(including yourself) that may be affecting the overall morale of your team?

- **Lack of interest or challenges**: Is a general lack of challenge or accountability contributing to increased complacency?
- **Competitive environment:** Is the competitive level of the environment dampening motivation—counter to our traditional expectations regarding competition in a sales environment?
- **Stress and pressure to perform**: Is your current management style or attitude, combined with your own stress levels, creating undue pressure or stress that is demotivating rather than inspiring?
- **Family problems:** Are family relationships, illnesses, or personal problems affecting an employee's ability to perform?
- **Depression:** Does an employee show signs of depression (this is a real and increasingly common factor)?
- **Change:** Do you perceive a resistance, struggle, or difficulty adapting to change?
- **Values are disrespected:** Do employees perceive that they're valued?

Every individual has his own value system. Values such as trust, respect, work ethic, and integrity are strong. If an employee feels these values are not respected, their motivation can be severely impacted, and in many cases, they will likely revolt or eventually change jobs. Perhaps an individual highly values workplace respect and professional behavior, in the midst of co-workers or even managers who do not share or embody those qualities. Such a situation is a motivation killer.

Remember, you can influence and affect others' actions, but motivation comes from within. When trying to motivate others, consider what you can do to influence and affect a person's actions, rather than simply asking, "How do I motivate them?"

Changing how we communicate, our management system, and leadership style can have significant impact on how others will respond and react. Sometimes when we want others to change, we may need to change.

Put It into Real-Life Practice

Consider a particular individual whose attitude and behavior you would like to influence. Collect a list of thoughts and ideas on great ways to motivate based on the following:

What are their "wants," their specific goals?

Why is it so important? What need does it satisfy?

How can you influence their attitude and motivation?

The best example I can provide is when a boss of mine knew that outside of work, my kids were extremely important to me. I wanted to be able to provide for them, be a positive role model, and maintain a better work/life balance. I recall arriving back in the office at 4:00 p.m., after a three-day work trip; my boss came into my office and said, "The numbers looks great for the month; you've been traveling and away from home most of the week. Please go home now, and take the girls to dinner on the corporate card as a thank you for all of your hard work and effort." I'm not sure if he actually knew how much that motivated me, or how intentional it was, but I was high for six months. He probably got even more work out of me, because of his actions. It satisfied all the needs above, but it was tailored specifically to me and what I wanted and needed.

Self-Reflection

An effective manager/coach reflects on his or her own performance, doesn't blame others, and always entertains the possibility that some of his or her actions or communications may contribute to problems a team member may be having. Ask yourself, "Would I want to work for me?" "Am I a good role model?" A particular coaching style that may have been effective at one stage in the development of the organization, or with a particular set of team members, may no longer necessarily be effective as business conditions change.

A great example of this is Tom Coughlin, head coach of the New York Giants football team. Coach Coughlin was well known for his old school, authoritarian approach to head coaching. With regard to his teams, his authority was absolute, and his approach to each of his players was strict and unyielding. Over time, Coughlin's approach drew increasingly sharp criticism from both players and team fans. He seemed disconnected from his players, insensitive to their particular needs as individuals, and subsequently out of step with many of the changes taking place in professional football in the modern era.

But then something happened. Coughlin changed his coaching

style. As many of the Giant's players stated, Coughlin's improved relationship with them inspired them to play harder for him and fight for the team. Not only did the changes in his coaching style improve his relationship with his players, it also demonstrated to them his commitment to winning: that achieving success was more important than stubbornly clinging to an old-fashioned coaching style. It brought the team closer together and created the emotional connections so important for true success. Coughlin was willing to change his approach and, in the end, attained the highest achievement in his profession and his career: his team overcame incredible odds and won the Super Bowl.

How did he do it? He made a larger effort to connect with his players on a personal level. He made it a priority to let his players know he was not just a coach, but also a human being. He listened to their concerns. He even took his team bowling during the pre-season. He created a leadership council of veteran players that would create better communication among the coaching staff and the players. Tom Coughlin's metamorphosis and the Giants' success underscores the importance of connecting with others and the impact it has on individual and team success.

Whether you're the business owner or sales executive, connecting with your employees on a personal level is an essential component of leadership. A coaching style of management will help you achieve this. Remember, a coach will make time for his or her people; a coach will listen to them, understand them, and let them know he or she cares. If Tom Coughlin can change at age sixty-one, then so can we. Ask yourself: Who do I need to connect with to enhance our team's success? What actions can I take today that will improve my relationships with my sales team? What can I do to have more of a coaching style of management?

There's no doubt that a coaching style of leadership is going to have positive implications on your team and your company. This starts at the top of organizations and can permeate positively throughout the company by training managers to have a coaching style as well.

The results will be increased productivity and financial goals being met. You'll improve job satisfaction, reduce stress, and improve morale. By spending more time and paying more attention to your employees, you'll naturally maximize their skills and talents, while decreasing turnover. All of a sudden, you're creating a team of champions, attracting the best talent, and staying competitive in building a bench. You're well on your way to amazing!

· ·

Coach Approach to Leadership Checklist

☐ Plan time together to get to know and understand your team.

☐ Create reflection questions as a tool for better understanding.

☐ Understand motivation and how you can influence others.

☐ Begin asking, not telling.

☐ Be conscientious about using open-ended questions to get dialogue going.

☐ Be authentic and present when listening.

☐ Self-reflect and make the necessary changes.

CHAPTER 10—COMMUNICATIONS

"The effectiveness of communication isn't defined
by the communication, but by the response."

—Milton Erickson

If improving your communication skills is an area of concentration for you, I suggest focusing on a few simple rules, along with understanding a communications model that can be applied in most situations.

Be approachable and accessible. You can do this by being physically and mentally present. Try walking around the office and engaging with your employees. To be present, practice being an active listener. Give your employees the time and attention they deserve. The next time they come into your office, ask them to have a seat, and then turn away from your computer, ignore your phone—be engaging and *listen*.

Do the same when communicating over the phone and let them know that you're physically moving away from your computer. There's nothing worse than them hearing you typing away as you're listening to them.

Share the credit and shoulder the blame. Many so-called leaders are distrusted today because they're seen as self-serving, primarily interested in their own benefits. Leadership should be for the benefit of the people. The biggest mistake you can make is to focus on "me," rather than your customers and the company. Get in the habit of saying *us, we* or *the team*; rather than *I.*

Thank people for their contributions. Everyone needs to know that they're appreciated. A "thank you" and recognition from the leader can go a long way. I have a thank you card from a former boss of mine pinned up in my office, seventeen years later.

Show you care. Employees want to work for leaders that are empathetic and genuinely concerned about their views and challenges. You can do this by showing and communicating your appreciation and respect for them. Begin involving them in the planning stages, rather than just telling them what to do.

Honor your commitments. Trust is imperative for leaders and their relationships. Do what you say you're going to do. Be consistent and predictable in your communications and behavior. Return phone calls and email communications in a timely fashion.

Have a sense of humor. Don't take yourself and others too seriously. Stay positive, smile, laugh, and have fun! A good sense of humor and laughter are wonderful tools in leadership communication.

Self-reflect. It's obvious that great leadership is the secret to retaining employees and achieving results. We need to always be self-reflecting, to make sure we are not overlooking what we can do better or different. Ask yourself, "In what areas do I need the most work?" Then, chart your course to work on improving what you do each day; incremental improvements become exponential over time.

Sometimes managers contribute to direct reports' problems and the cause for poor working relations or lack of communication. Ask yourself if you're part of the problem, and do some self-reflecting and evaluation of your communications style toward the other person.

Consider the following questions:

Am I using my own performance and values to set expectations or to judge others? You've probably progressed in your career by setting high expectations and achieving an outstanding track record. Assuming that others have identical motivations or identical strengths may result in your putting your values onto them, which could be unrealistic.

I remember as a young sales leader, I was furious when my sales reps would leave right at 5:00 p.m. I couldn't understand how they could watch the clock, leave their work behind, and be done for the day. At the time, I didn't have a family to attend to, and my life was pretty much centered on my career.

I soon realized that when I had exaggerated expectations of

others, I would be disappointed. I also found that putting my work ethic on them was not motivating at all. I was able to help them get the job done in other ways.

Have I passed up chances to listen? People don't always know what kind of help they need or exactly how to ask for it. When you see an opportunity, take the time to listen actively, ask open-ended questions, and get dialogue and an open conversation going. When you're actively listening; you can easily uncover needs and identify additional coaching opportunities. Always having the answers, and telling others what to do is a trap that many busy managers fall into. The next time someone is standing at your door with a question, don't pass up the opportunity to ask them what they think… and listen.

Would I want to work for me? This is a deep one. Are there certain things you would not like about working for you? Remember, you're the leader and it's important to be a role model for those that work for you. For example, if you view good communication skills as important in cultivating good teamwork, then model those skills every chance you get.

We often see leaders reading all of the self-help books and quoting the leadership gurus, but not walking the walk. Sometimes it is hard to look in the mirror, and justify why you might be a certain way.

Is it hard for me to identify with someone? Be self-aware and recognize when your own feelings, such as anger, frustration, or judgment may keep you from appreciating how someone else is feeling. Having empathy is necessary to fully understanding others' ideas or feelings, so you can begin to identify with them. Being empathetic, when it doesn't come natural, is difficult. It requires thinking more with your heart, and not just your head and gut.

Am I avoiding the situation or problem? Avoidance is an easy thing to do. Addressing a crucial conversation can be a lot more painful, making it easy to prolong that conversation. When you prolong a crucial conversation, you'll only prolong the undesired behavior.

Feedback

Leaders may not realize the importance of providing feedback to their employees to enhance organizational growth and development. When correctly given, feedback helps improve job performance while promoting professional and personal growth in employees. Often this isn't something that many of us think about during our hectic, daily, business lives. Providing feedback offers many benefits, and when given at the right time, with the right constructive and positive message, it can yield great results.

Providing feedback can improve employee morale and reduce confusion regarding expectations and current performance. Think of feedback as guidance that will enable your employee to learn as well as improve the quality of his or her work. You'll also see a difference in how feedback enhances your interpersonal relationship with your employees.

There are two forms of feedback you can provide: positive feedback and constructive feedback. Positive feedback is used to reinforce desired behavior. Constructive feedback addresses areas in need of improvement. It's important to provide employees with both forms of feedback in order to improve and maintain quality performance.

Providing Positive Feedback

Let's explore an example of giving positive feedback. What can you do to be more effective and to ensure your employees continue the positive behavior that you want from them?

For example, after a successful sales call with your sales rep, you get in the car and say, "You did a great job! Way to go!" In your mind, you might think that you're encouraging them and giving them positive feedback, right? Consider the following steps as a means to praise as well as reinforce excellent performance:

Describe the positive behavior. "I thought you did a great job on the sales call. You were asking the customer a lot of important, open-ended questions to understand what they need, rather than just talking about price and telling them about our company."

Explain why the behavior is positive. "This was important because you were able to build rapport; they opened up and told us a lot of important information about their current situation that will enable us to come back with a winning proposal."

Help the individual accept credit. "Do you understand why this was so great? You really applied some great selling skills."

Thank and encourage the individual. "I just wanted to thank you for your efforts. If you continue these types of selling skills, you'll have a lot of success in getting new accounts and growing your business."

The example shows how a few more sentences added to the typical "Way to go!" can more clearly communicate the impact of the positive behavior, and can ensure they continue it in the future for long-term results.

Providing Constructive Feedback

At K.Coaching, we work with many clients who want to improve their leadership and communications skills. Often we see managers avoiding crucial conversations or giving negative feedback. Sometimes it may feel better to just ignore the situation, hoping that it will go away, instead of addressing the situation appropriately and constructively. Most likely, the manager will provide short, pointed, unflattering remarks to get a sales rep's attention.

The next time an employee requires constructive feedback, consider the opportunity for you to make a positive impact on future behavior through direction and meaningful advice. If given properly, constructive feedback can make a difference between an employee's success and failure, since its purpose is to improve their job performance.

Consider the following example and steps as an effective process for giving constructive feedback: You have a sales rep who isn't spending enough time in the field; you constantly see them at their desk, seemingly busy, but not meeting your expectations and certainly not visiting enough prospects or current clients.

What you might say: "What are you still doing in the office?"

Or, worse, "Is your car broken?" Maybe you'll ask, "Don't you have any sales calls today?" Or, like many people often do, you'll just ignore it, complain to someone else, or go back to your office and stew about it, letting your frustration build. Obviously, none of these responses are constructive, nor will they communicate your expectations or yield different results.

Instead, try this approach:

Identify the problem behavior. "I'd like to talk with you a moment; please come into my office. I've noticed that you've been in the office, rather than in front of customers, and this is a problem. Your responsibility is to spend 50 percent of your time on face-to-face appointments with customers and prospects, and you're not doing that."

Explain how the behavior is wrong or detrimental. "The reason this is so critical is that we are in a very competitive market and your current customers are being prospected by our competitors. You need to stay close with them and always be providing value. We have talked about you having at least two prospect appointments a day to bring in the new business we are expecting of you."

Help the individual acknowledge the problem. "Do you understand why this is a problem, and that it needs to be corrected?" This should not be a one-way conversation. Ask them some open-ended questions to get them talking and "owning" the problem. Ask specific questions to better understand their position on the problem. Remember to begin your open-ended questions with, "Tell me about" or "Describe to me," so you don't receive one-word answers.

Develop goals with the individual. "Let's agree on some goals to get you on a schedule for being in the field during certain times of the day. Let's also develop a clearer understanding of the amount of time you should allocate to face-to-face customer meetings compared to time spent in the office." Ask them what they think, and have them come up with their own realistic and attainable goals, such as, "What hours of the day can you carve out?" "How many days a week can you commit to?" "What can I do better to help you?"

Monitor the individual's performance. "I'd like to meet with you every Friday at 4:00 p.m. to review your weekly activities and success in this area. I'm sure that if you keep up this new schedule, you'll meet your sales goals and have a great year!"

A Few Tips on Feedback

- Managers should only give feedback to improve an employee's job performance or work-related behavior. Feedback should not be given regarding an employee's private life unless it affects their ability to work.
- Focus on the individual's actions rather than their personality.
- Focus on the individual's future instead of dwelling on past actions.
- For the greatest impact, don't delay feedback. Provide it as soon as possible after you become aware of problem behavior.

- Give accurate details to prevent the individual from misunderstanding your feedback.
- Learn the individual's point of view to gain insight into his or her behavior.
- Make sure you give feedback in a private setting—especially the constructive feedback.
- Document your feedback, regardless of how insignificant it may seem.

Being an effective manager and sales leader isn't easy, but taking the time to practice giving constructive and positive feedback can get you on your way to great personal progress and team success.

Delegating

Many individuals have a hard time delegating tasks. They tend to think that they can do it themselves better and faster than someone else. Often it's difficult to give up the control, especially if you're not confident in the ability of others.

If you want to make a significant difference managing your time, you must begin to delegate. But learning how to delegate effectively is the key. Once you master this form of communication, you'll no longer be disappointed in the outcomes, and start to hand off even more time-consuming and critical tasks.

One of the best practices to begin delegation is to review the list of your to-dos and write a person's name beside them, which you could possibly delegate to. You'll likely discover that there are certain tasks you can and should delegate and it's important to understand why you aren't. There may be even bigger issues to address than you just not delegating enough. I like to think of delegation as a three-step process to ensure the other person is very clear on the expectation and is ready and willing to take ownership.

1. Clearly define the task at hand and gain their understanding of the value of the job, to the business and for them personally. Any task or project you want to be completed may come naturally to you, yet it's important to communicate the task very clearly, not leaving out any details. It is vital to state the value and necessity of the task or project. When you describe the value, the other person will feel as though you trust them and will know the task is important to you and to the organization. Sometimes without this, they may feel as though you're "dumping" something onto them, or it's menial work.

2. Establish expectations for the quality of work and the specific deliverables, and answer any questions to eliminate confusion. Communicate what the final outcome should look like. There is no room for mind-reading. This is your chance to show them what "good" looks like. What exactly is the format you want it in? An email, Excel sheet, presentation? Show them an example of what you have in mind. Make sure you check for "buy-in" and acceptance. This may be a simple confirmation back to you that they understand, and accept the project or task. This isn't, "Do you understand?" or "Do you have any questions?" In order to truly ensure understanding, ask them questions like, "What do you think about XYZ or describe to me…"

3. Set a specific date and time deadline and/or agree on a status update. Be clear and specific and don't use timelines like "by tomorrow afternoon" or "before the end of the day." Rather be clear and specific such as "1:00 p.m. tomorrow," or "by Tuesday the 5th."

This delegation process may seem obvious and simple, but once you practice this with real situations, you'll see how powerful it can be, and soon it will become a habit. Any delegation is best done during face-to-face communications, but can be adapted for email or remote management.

Race to Amazing Conversation Model

Having a consistent coaching style of leadership isn't easy and certainly takes a fair amount of practice. The best way to become proficient in your coaching style is to have consistency in how you have coaching conversations. Your coaching skills are very similar to muscles. The more you use them, the stronger they become.

The Race to Amazing Conversation Model is a great way to begin developing and teaching you how to have more effective conversations with all level of employees and positions.

It's important to listen to their story and work closely with them as individuals. Ask questions so you can better understand their obstacles, while using your head, heart, and gut. You should not make assumptions, have preconceived notions, or be just looking for specific business results.

During the conversation, let the idea for the resolution to the challenge or problem be theirs. Collaborate with them and work together to determine the action steps or specific goals that they want to achieve. The key words here are that *they* want to achieve, not just what you're expecting.

Below is a breakdown of the Race to Amazing Conversation Model with key elements to guide you.

Step 1: Clearly Understand the Situation

Don't assume you have a complete understanding of the situation. Allow the other person to fully express themselves. Listen attentively, look for nonverbal cues, and ask open-ended questions to create dialogue and clarity.

Examples:

"Tell me more about that."
"Why was that important to you?"
"How were you feeling about…"

Step 2: Gain Mutual Awareness

Begin helping them discover possible resolutions by sharing experiences rather than giving your advice or opinion. Listen to their words, then summarize and paraphrase the themes that come to the surface. Repeat back to them the core message you're hearing, and specifically ask what some possibilities or resolutions might be.

Examples:

"If I heard you correctly..."
"What are some possibilities?"
"What are your top three options?"

Step 3: Agree on Action Plan

Facilitate the discussion around creating goals and the action plan. Help them prioritize the goals and define realistic timelines. Come to a mutual agreement on the next steps and how you'll measure success.

Examples:

"What do you see as your next steps?"
"When will you have that completed?"
"How will you measure success?"

No matter who you're having a conversation with, you can turn it into a coaching conversation by fully understanding the situation, identifying gaps, and collectively coming up with a solution. Once you master this Race to Amazing Conversation Model you'll find it helpful not only with employees, but also with customers, prospects, and business partners.

It takes certain coaching skills that surround the Race to

Amazing Conversation Model, beginning with being present and ending with goal-setting.

Race to Amazing Coaching Skills

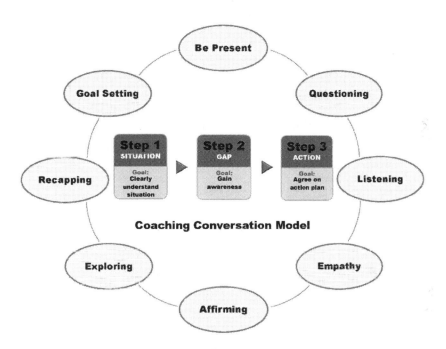

Coaching Conversation Model

Below are the definitions of the coaching skills to have an effective coaching conversation. This in itself takes a great deal of practice, but use this model as your guide.

Race to Amazing Coaching Skills Definitions

Being present: Give full attention, keep an open posture, and maintain eye contact.

Questioning: Ask open and closed-ended questions; avoid leading questions.

Listening: Be quiet and attentive; paraphrase/summarize accurately.

Showing empathy: Show interest, concern, and an emotional connection.

Affirming: Recognize and affirm the person's strengths and achievements.

Exploring: Facilitate brainstorming to help discover, analyze, and prioritize.

Recapping: Accurately summarize the person's situation, feelings, and next steps.

Goal Setting: Facilitate action plans, goals, and measurements for success.

CHAPTER 11—KEYS TO AMAZING RESULTS

"If your actions create a legacy that inspires
others to dream more, learn more, do more and become
more, then, you are an excellent leader."

— Dolly Parton

If this is your first pass at learning more about effective sales leadership, you may be feeling overwhelmed by now. Even the best of the best need to hone skills and be constantly learning. Throughout your Race to Amazing, it has been about you and what you can do better or different to get the results you're looking for. I've introduced leadership development and awareness activities, a successful management system, go-to-market strategy models, and how to develop a coaching style of leadership. In this chapter, I'll break it down and highlight the keys to consistent amazing sales results.

Win with People

Having the right people in the right seats will make your life easier and help you reach your goals faster. Your position is designed to motivate and inspire, so you can get the performance results through others. You also need to address and manage the under-performers. Even the best sales leaders in the world won't get the results they desire if they have the wrong people.

Winning with people also means recognizing that you can't do it alone, that you need a team of people, and that you must trust and believe in those that work for you and with you. Building teams is an art and talent of its own. Effectively leading and managing managers is another level and skill set. It takes constant awareness, at all levels of the organization, of what "people talent" is needed or missing to fill gaps or build a bench.

Salespeople tend to be easier to evaluate than other employees because their performance is usually tied to a specific quota or goal, and that number determines the level of their success. If they have the basic skills and the motivation, you may want to continue to invest in their development.

I like to use the simple ABC ranking method, which you can do for any of your employees. List the employees that you're directly responsible for, and rank them as an A, B, or C Player:

A Player: Meets their financial and/or performance commitment to the organization. For salespeople, it's a quota achievement. For others, it would be performance goals or metrics, and meeting expectations for continuous development, good corporate citizenship, and being a team player with the right attitude.

B Player: Meets one or the other. Maybe they're meeting their numbers, but they're not a team player or have a bad attitude. Or maybe they're a great corporate citizen, really putting forward the effort and want to do well, but they're just not meeting their performance goals.

C Player: Meets neither of the above two criteria.

With this simple review you can then determine where you need to invest your time and attention to get the B's up to A's, and how you'll deal with the C's by providing feedback, coaching, and performance planning.

Investment Criteria

After you determine your A, B, and C players, it's important to understand the developmental needs of each. Then determine whether they're worth your investment of time and resources. This exercise will quickly help you to determine where you need to invest your time and resources into further development or begin to assess their value and future potential.

One way to do that is to rate an employee's coachability factors and determine the necessary amount of investment:

Coachability: Able to learn and change.

Insight: Demonstrates an understanding of his or her strengths, weaknesses, and impact on others.

Motivation: Seeks feedback, responds constructively (not defensively) to feedback, and changes his or her behavior in response to feedback.

Basic Skills: Possesses the fundamental skills required to do the job.

Interviewing and Selecting

In today's competitive sales environments, you need to have a fresh, new breed of polished and professional sales reps facing your customers. Yet, finding and retaining high quality sales professionals is one of the biggest challenges facing many companies today. The talent pool is the best it's ever been. Don't wait until you have an opening. Finding and retaining great people should be an ongoing process—and a commitment to excellence for your organization.

If you don't have the luxury of outsourcing your recruitment, or have an HR department to help with the selection process, this task often lands on the business owner or sales leader's lap. Detail the position you're looking to fill, including the required knowledge, job responsibilities, skills, and core competencies. This makes it easier to identify and appeal to candidates who possess the qualifications or characteristics best-suited to your organization's needs and culture. Have a job description, interview questions to understand the candidate's core competencies, and an assessment process and tool to measure their capacity for the job requirements. As a company, you should define the core competencies you're looking for and create standard behavioral questions to target that competency during the interview process.

Core Competency—Prospecting Skills

These days, all salespeople need honed prospecting skills to be assertive and proactive in getting new accounts and closing business. If the sales rep doesn't have any prospecting experience, you must be willing to take a risk and also invest in personal one-on-one time and professional training to prepare them for success in landing new accounts.

Remember, having sales experience doesn't necessarily mean they're good at prospecting. The interview isn't about likability and going with your gut, but rather, whether the candidate possesses the traits to succeed in the position. Interviewing around core competencies will eliminate both the impostors and the too nice guys.

Use interview questions that hone in on discovering whether they possess the skills that you need. As an example, the interview questions below are designed to learn more about the candidates prospecting skills and abilities:

- Tell me about your experience in cold calling on prospect accounts for your company.
- Tell me about a time you were able to bring on a difficult new account.
- What was your new business quota and what did you achieve?
- What was the sales process and how did you get the new account?

When you interview specifically for the competencies, you'll quickly see whether they possess the required skills and how much you'll need to invest in additional training and development. This approach also ensures that you're not just interviewing from their resume and often takes them off-guard, if they're expecting standard interview questions and are prepared with canned answers.

Provide Quality Training, Orientation, and Onboarding

The first day on the job should be their best day. I remember showing up for my first day at work, where I was given a dusty desk with coffee stains, and it was sitting in the hallway—not the best first impression. I've also witnessed new employees on their first day and I'm scratching my head, because they seem totally different than how they were in the interview. That's why first day and week observations are so important, and why many companies have a ninety-day probationary period, to ensure that you're a good fit for each other.

Make their first days really count. Spend time with them, take them to lunch, and make them feel welcome. Share the company vision and how they will be an integral part of both the team and the company's success. Then share your expectations for them in terms of performance and results. Make sure you review in detail the written goals and objectives. Have a conversation early on about how they will be measured, held accountable, and rewarded.

Create a well-defined onboarding program with clearly defined, realistic first-year employee expectations for learning and development. Be personally committed to the resources and time required to make the sales rep successful, regardless of their past experience.

Experienced sales professionals are always selling, and they will sell you. Don't let them hide their deficiencies, or "spin sell" the results. Don't let them convince you that "they got this." Everyone needs direction, management, and further development to be a better salesperson.

You need to be providing sales skills training, regardless of the salesperson's experience or age. It's often the veteran or the old pro who thinks they don't need it, and yet typically it's them who need it the most. Every sales professional, whether they're a new hire or not, needs to understand what is expected of them, that the company is also investing in them, and there's a roadmap to succeed.

Have a Sales Process

A successful sales process is a proven, documented sales approach with messaging and job aids that represent your winning model for gaining, penetrating, and retaining accounts. A formal process would include standardized scripts that ensure everyone is saying the same things, conveying the same message to customers, and is supported by consistent job aids and marketing tools that are appropriately aligned to the steps and activities in the process.

Sales reps appreciate a standardized process because it helps them be more efficient, develop stronger skills through repetition, and spares them from having to reinvent the wheel with every prospect or opportunity. When they get stuck in pursuit of an opportunity, a process provides them guidance with suggested next steps, instead of leaving them floundering and feeling stalled in their efforts.

Sales reps also gain a sense of company commitment, support, and dedication toward the sales department and their efforts. But the greatest satisfaction—for both the company and its sales reps—comes when they see the true outcomes of being more professional and closing more accounts faster.

Once the process is defined, it's easier to manage the sales funnel and the expectations surrounding sales activities. A process creates a system of accountability to new business and better information for estimating new cash flow. Managers can also determine where in the sales process the sales reps are getting stuck so they can address these issues sooner rather than later. Sales reps' problems are often the result of not giving the appropriate amount of effort, or their selling style or methods aren't effective; a process takes the guesswork out of the latter, and allows a manager to manage the sales reps behavior and activities accordingly. Then the results will come.

Create Your Power Statement

 You may be familiar with the terms "power messaging" or "power statements," but unclear on what they can do for your business success or your brand. Imagine everyone in your company answering the question "What do you do?" in the same manner and with a compelling powerful message that will resonate with your prospects and customers—a message so strong that it will motivate and inspire them to take action.

I would like to define five simple steps in creating your power message, so you can work on this to boost your sales effectiveness and results.

1. **Define who you are.** The first step is to think deeply and reflect about who you're as a company, what is your purpose, your cause, your belief? If you're a company without purpose, cause, or beliefs, well, you're just another company. A power message starts with *why* you do what you do. Once you've identified your philosophy and your purpose, you'll communicate that in a unique way and begin to think, act,

and communicate from the inside out. To understand the *why* concept, I encourage you to listen to Simon Sinek's TED Talk, Starting With WHY. He is a popular author and highly sought-after speaker on the subject of how great leaders inspire action through starting with why. As Sinek notes, "People don't buy *what* you do; they buy *why* you do it!" A power message should be easily understood, short and memorable, yet communicate your company's focus and passion very clearly to your customers. Once you create your power message, you can repurpose it in many ways and use it as part of your company's branding strategy.

2. **Define your client.** The second step is to define your target market. Who will be listening to your message? Below is a list of questions to help you define your ideal client. Not only will this give you greater clarity for profiling and targeting, but it will help you better understand how they think, what their needs are, and how they make decisions. This thoughtful exercise will help you craft your power message to appeal specifically to them, in a clear concise manner.

> *Who are current and potential clients?*
> *What do they look like?*
> *How do they think?*
> *What is important to them, as a company?*
> *What are their needs?*
> *How do they make decisions?*

3. **Write the message.** Now that you've better defined your customer, begin crafting your message. Below is a format to

follow as you describe *what* you do, *who* you do it for, *how* you do it (better than anyone else), and the *impact* that your customer will feel by doing business with you. Don't forget to add your *why,* which should be positioned at the beginning of the power statement. This message is about you, but should be written in the third person or what we call the *you* language. When a customer or prospect hears your message, they should feel as though it's directed specifically to them and they feel emotionally connected to it.

It should include the following:

- **WHAT** do you do?
- **WHO** is your target?
- **HOW** do you do it?
- What is the **IMPACT** that you'll have, or what are the actionable results they will receive from you?
- Most important, include your **WHY.**

For demonstration purposes, below is an example of our company's power statement without the **WHY**, targeted market or impact. After that, is an example that includes the **WHY** with a stronger emphasis on **HOW**, with more "what it means to them," and includes an emotional appeal.

Power Statement #1 – "K.Coaching is **(WHAT)** *a coaching, consulting and training organization.* We help **(WHO)** *companies improve their sales strategies, processes, and leadership.*"

Where is the WHY, HOW, and IMPACT?

Power Statement #2 – (WHY) *"We believe in the power and impact that effective sales leadership has on organizations and are passionate about helping individuals and companies grow. Your industry is ever changing and remains highly competitive, but there is no need for you to do it alone.*

K.Coaching has helped *(WHO) hundreds of companies, sales leaders and their teams (WHAT) realize their full potential.* We do this *(HOW) through our* Race to Amazing *Program, which offers leadership development, easy to execute sales strategies, proven processes, and successful sales management systems that will get you on the fast track to sales success.*

(IMPACT) With Race to Amazing, *you'll make the changes needed to get the best results through others, become the amazing leader you know you can be, and lead your life with passion and purpose."*

Both example messages are about the same company, with the same capabilities. Which one resonated with you? Which one would you be more interested in exploring? That is the power of messaging, and a good reason to put the time and effort into creating yours.

4. **Repurpose the message.** Once you get the basic components of your message written, then it becomes very easy to repurpose in other forms. Make sure that your sales organization can practice and deliver the message with ease and adapt it to various situations. Be sure to include your

message and the "YOU" language on your website and marketing materials to better connect with your prospective or current customers. You can begin to speak your customer's language through social media, while being recognized in your community as an industry leader and expert.

5. **Begin using it.** There are many benefits to taking this to market and using it as part of your branding strategy. Everyone will have the same approach with no misunderstandings. You'll find your employees have a clear understanding of the company's purpose and mission and how they fit into the big picture. It will naturally foster a team environment, enhance morale, and greatly improve the business focus.

As you can see, a power message can be a powerful thing and it's way more than an elevator pitch. Take the time to craft it for your company and see it create a life of its own as you make it a part of your culture, brand and future sales and marketing plans.

Become an Executive Sponsor

If you're not establishing high-level relationships at the executive level with top customers, you're making a huge mistake. You should be known by all of your key accounts as the Executive Sponsor. Do not allow your sales reps to be the only ones with significant customer relationships. Your customers, at the executive level, need to know you personally, value the partnership you have with them, and see you as a trusted advisor.

If you don't take action and begin building these important executive relationships, you'll find yourself in a bind if a sales rep leaves or you need to let them go. Customer retention and loyalty are too critical to your success and the overall success of the sales organization for you not to be involved.

Check and Recheck the Seven Steps to Sales Success

If you're looking for amazing sales results year over year, use our Seven Steps to Sales Success proven method for building a successful and sustainable sales organization. The steps in this model have been well explained throughout *Race to Amazing*. Check and recheck to make sure year-over-year you're making each step solid to achieve the best sales results for your organization.

Read through the model, below, to determine on a scale of 1 to 5 (five being the highest score) where you would place the strength of your steps in the current year. Then determine what you can do better or different during your business planning and execution of your plans for the upcoming year.

When you review the model, keep in mind the order of the steps are important; with the first step being the foundation and the subsequent steps building from the ones that came before it. In my experience, companies will have most of the steps, but some steps are weaker than others. In many cases, businesses will skip steps altogether, or not realize the many components of that step and their importance:

1. **Mission/vision/passion (MVP).** What are your company's mission, vision, and passion? Where does it reside? Are they on

a website, in your head, or in the hearts and minds of all of your employees and customers? Employees want to know they're working for a business that has a purpose, a plan, and vision for the future. What is your *why*? Why are you doing what you're doing every day? What drives you? Are your dreams, realities, guiding principles, and core values well established and understood by all?

2. Build your go-to-market strategy. Once you have a clear picture of your *why* and your ultimate outcomes, it's now time to begin a deeper dive into your company, the competition, and the industry. Understand your strengths, weaknesses, opportunities, and threats by doing a SWOT analysis every year. Understand what is happening in your market. What is the competition doing? Where and how is your current business growing? What are the changes and needs of the customers?

3. Get tactical with the CPR model. After you've done this discovery, you want to play from a position of strength and build a tactical plan around what you can realistically accomplish within a given period of time. Where is your business weak as it pertains to the business trends of growth and attrition? Then, determine what the tactical game plan should be. Prioritize your activities based on what will make you the most money, can be implemented the easiest, at the lowest costs. We suggest looking at activities in the three areas: conversion (new business), penetration (selling more to existing accounts), and retention (creating customer loyalty). When you have all these tactical plans being executed simultaneously, your business will grow.

4. Clearly define and communicate. Once you know the "what to do," it's time to put the meat on the bone and clearly define and communicate the go-to-market strategy and CPR Game Plan. We suggest creating a company DOGOM as a means of documenting each strategy in a clear and concise fashion, so that you can best communicate, execute, and lead your game plan. Describe the strategy. What are the objectives? List the specific goals. Who is the owner and how will you measure and monitor for accountability? Your management system and sales process should be communicated. Each sales rep should be aligned to the company plan with their individual expectations and objectives as well as tactics tied to goals and quotas.

5. Measure and monitor accountability. Often companies are weak in Steps 4 and 5, and then the plans and strategies don't get executed and led through the sales team. Everyone gets busy and is seemingly working hard, but without team and individual accountability, the best-laid plans fall apart. We suggest monthly one-on-ones for individual accountability and regular team sales meetings to reinforce company strategy. Regular score-boarding against quotas and expectations should be done while creating a culture of comradery and fun.

6. Develop and motivate. Unfortunately, this is the step that often gets forgotten. The sales organization may have all of the above steps intact, but the sales reps are then left to fend for themselves; be self-motivated and expected to learn and develop along the way. Begin this step with score-boarding your reps as an A, B, or C player. This should be based on the competencies needed to be successful in their position. Are they meeting their sales quotas? Are they a team player with the right attitude? Then you can build a developmental plan along with them for continuous improvement. This step should include reward and recognition, motivation by listening and understanding while coaching and driving the behavior that you want… because they want to do it.

7. Leadership with PUC. This is the most crucial step of all. You may have all of the previous steps, but without effective leadership you'll ultimately fail. Leadership with PUC is leading with passion, urgency, and commitment. It is about having an inspiring positive attitude and fearless focus. This is the style in which to lead the system that you've created in the previous steps.

Now that you've scored your company's effectiveness in each of these steps on a scale of one to five, reflect back on this year and previous ones. Would strengthening a particular step have yielded better results? What needs to change? What will you do now to best prepare for a successful new year?

 Seven Steps to Sales Success Exercise

After you've scored on a scale of 1 to 5 the above seven steps, indicate what areas you'll be focused on for improvements.

Set an action plan with timelines to address areas for improvement.

CHAPTER 12—SHIPBUILDING

"All lasting business is built on friendship."

—Alfred A. Montapert

You're almost at the finish line. It's time to take a breather, step back, and review your original objectives for your Race to Amazing found in Chapter 3. Are you on course or have you taken a different path?

There's so much to learn about ourselves and what we can possibly do better or different to change our personal and professional outcome. In life, your Race to Amazing is a constant journey. Is there really a finish line? Sure you want to experience that amazing feeling of "I have arrived." But it's the journey that is the most fun! Along your journey, you'll find that the greatest rewards are the positive results and impact you can have on your personal and professional relationships.

At the end of the race, isn't it all about the human race and what really matters?

 This became apparent to me during the early stages of my coaching practice when I was working with Jim, a sales executive for a medium-size business. One of his coaching objectives was to improve his relationships with his sales team. He had eight sales reps reporting to him, but they were reluctant to take him on calls because he wasn't very effective, yet that was a big part of his role and responsibility. He would actually embarrass them by talking too much and completely hijacking the sales call. To his credit, he recognized this so he committed himself to improving and developing these skills.

His other coaching objective was to work on building relationships with business partners and high-level clients. He was the Executive Sponsor on those relationships, and he needed to carve out time to cultivate them.

We worked together for a number of months, and in one of our coaching sessions, he said, "Krista, I have the perfect prospect and I'd like to go on a sales call with one of my reps, and practice some of what I've been learning." I was excited for him until he told me who the client was. I asked, "Are you sure you want to practice your new skills on THIS guy?" I was concerned about how it might go. For the sake of the story let's call this prospect Grumpy—I knew he was going to be a bit of a challenge.

But Jim said, "Yes, I'm ready. Put me in, Coach." The next day he goes along with the sales rep on the call, and it went famously.

Jim sat back, he listened, didn't say a word; he let his sales rep run the meeting. The rep asked great open-ended questions, discovered the needs, aligned the solutions, and was getting ready to close the deal. Jim was just sitting there being very professional, very supportive. All of a sudden, Grumpy turns to him and says, "So, what do you do anyhow?" Jim was startled; he froze for a minute, and then sat back in his chair, unsure of what to say. On the wall behind Grumpy was a large photograph of Grumpy standing in front of a big fishing boat, and he was grinning from ear to ear. His arms were outstretched; he was holding a huge fish he had just caught. Jim was staring at the image; his eyes were locked on the wall over Grumpy's head, trying to think of how to respond. Grumpy asked again, "Well, whatcha do?" Jim then said, "I build ships." Grumpy says, "Whaddya mean you build ships?" Jim said, "I build ships. I build partnerships and I build relationships." Well, it was at that point that Grumpy and Jim started building their ship together.

When Jim called me after that meeting and told me the story, I thought it was brilliant thinking and a major breakthrough for both of them. Since then, with Jim's permission, I've taken the whole shipbuilding concept, began studying and researching key elements of building ships – partnerships and relationships.

I'm pleased to share with you the shipbuilding concept as part of your journey to Race to Amazing. I think we'd all agree that our relationships with our business partners, customers, and employees can make the difference between a successful business and one that isn't growing. I'd like to challenge your thinking and consider that it's not just because you have these relationships that your business will prosper, but that you continuously nurture them. If you intentionally, deliberately, and proactively work on building your "ships"—partnerships and relationships—you'll have sustainable growth.

When I started researching shipbuilding, I found over five hundred words that contain "ship," such as citizenship, stewardship, friendship, leadership—and the list goes on. The words all seemed positive and building something. Except for shipwreck—now that's what will happen if you don't take care of them!

I started going a little crazy with my theory and thinking that maybe we are our own ship; after all, our bodies are made up of 80 percent water. The health and strength of our partnerships and relationships can have a physical and emotional effect on how we feel in any given day. For example, if you have a business partner who owes you a phone call or maybe they were supposed to send you something and didn't, you're bothered by that and you feel uncomfortable.

From a personal perspective, if a relationship is a little shaky at home, or you're worried about your children, it's likely you bring that to the office and vice versa. Ultimately all of the "relationship turbulence" can be stressful and is affecting you, whether you realize it or not. Your personal ship isn't solid and you're not feeling purposeful.

What Does Your Ship Look Like?

I began wondering what my ship looks like. I certainly wanted it to be a big ship. Like the Titanic—a big, beautiful, glamorous ship. But does size really matter when it comes to ships? After all, the Titanic sank. No, but one thing is for sure: ships are built for a purpose and built solid to last a lifetime.

How does the shipbuilding concept correlate to you, to leadership, and to business? Think about the people you know that failed or companies that went bankrupt. Is it possible that because they weren't intentional and proactive on nurturing and building their relationships with their customers, or employees or business partnerships that they didn't succeed?

Shipbuilding means forging a professional and personal connection with key relationships and partnerships that matter to your success, and working together toward common long-term goals, whether that is customers, suppliers, employees, business partners and colleagues, or your family.

Let's explore what that really means, and discover how you can build your ships to last a lifetime.

Key Elements of Shipbuilding

I'd like you to think about one or two of the most important relationships or partnerships to your success and happiness. As you read through the key elements to shipbuilding, be thinking about those relationships in particular. This will help determine what areas you may need to focus on or nurture. This can be both professional and/or personal, as these key elements will apply in either case.

Understanding

In order to have a mutual understanding of each other's wants and needs, first you need to ask questions, listen, and discover what is happening in their business, or in their world. You may need to dig deep to discover the need behind the need. With understanding, there are no assumptions made, or anyone taken for granted. Once you have a mutual understanding of each other's wants and needs, you can determine the common goals and begin working toward achieving them together. This may make sense on a business level when you're dealing with customers or business partners. I want to share with you a more personal story.

Just Ask

One of the most important relationships to me growing up was the one I had with my grandmother, Grandma Betty. I was the oldest granddaughter and born on her birthday; that made for quite a special relationship. Over the years, I moved further and further away from my hometown and it was difficult to maintain that close relationship. I remember when she turned eighty. I wanted to do something special for her birthday. I asked my mother and my brothers what they thought about Grandma being interested in going to a spa for a day and night. They all said, "No way! She never leaves the house and she's never gone away without Poppa." Well, I asked her and to everyone's surprise she said, "Yes." I'll never forget the day I went to pick her up for our two-hour drive to Berkeley Springs, West Virginia, to the then Coolfont Resort. When I arrived at their small farmhouse on the end of Shady Lane, I was surprised that Grandma Betty wasn't sitting at the kitchen table, where she always was. My heart stopped. I thought something had happened to her or something was wrong. I asked Poppa, "Where's Grandma? Is everything OK? Is she ready and excited to go?" He said in his low, slow voice, "She's been ready for days." I then saw her come down the steps with her matching shoes and purse, in her Sunday best with a smile on her face. We were going to the spa!

Needless to say, we had a wonderful time. I remember sitting on the deck of our cabin, late at night, feet on the railing, while she smoked a cigarette and I smoked a cigar. We laughed for hours on end, as we shared childhood stories and reminisced about Christmas at Aunt Shinnie's, 1972.

I remember saying, "Grandma, I'm so happy that we're here and you agreed to come. Everyone I talked to said that you wouldn't, because you never leave the house." She said, "Well, no one ever asked me."

Please, just ask. If I had never asked, if I had assumed, then I wouldn't have experienced one of the most wonderful times of my life: celebrating my grandmother's eightieth birthday in such a special way.

Know Your Role and Your Purpose

Whether you're a father, grandparent, mom, boss, or employee, you play a role. You should be very clear on what that role is and your purpose in the relationship. As a business owner or sales manager, your role is to create and share your vision, build a business plan, and get results through others. Your employees are looking to you to be the "fearless leader." Are you playing that role? So often relationships get taken for granted, or you believe you're playing your role. I recall speaking about shipbuilding at a conference and afterward an older gentleman came up to me with tears in his eyes and said, "Thank you, I left the meeting and went and called my grandson. We're going fishing next week." It doesn't have to be complicated; that is shipbuilding.

What Value Do You Bring?

Ask yourself, "What value do I bring to this relationship and what areas do I need to work on?" If you do not bring value to the other person, then they may lose respect for you or emotionally disconnect in the relationship. Often, this results in a breakup or an employee leaving the company. Your relationships need to have value and purpose for each other. It can't be one-sided. Many marriages fail because one of the partners isn't meeting the needs of the other. In business, if you don't constantly ask yourself this question, complacency sets in and your customers may begin to question what value you bring to the relationship.

Reciprocity

If sometimes you feel like the other person isn't holding up their end of the bargain, and that you're always giving and they're taking; then there's no reciprocity. A partnership should not feel unfair, or be one-sided. Often reciprocity begins with good communications of each other's expectations and how you're feeling about your position in the partnership.

Grandma Betty used to say, "Kristy, there's givers and takers in life; you're either one or the other." It was a rather distorted way to go through life. I would look at people and think to myself,

"Giver, taker, he's a giver, she's a taker." But there is some merit to that. Imagine building a partnership when both people are takers? Reciprocity is a must for any successful partnership; make sure you're giving your all and getting it in return. When you're building your partnerships, be very clear up front on what the expectations are of each other.

More often than not, it's just a verbal understanding and you're communicating expectations and hoping the other person hears you and understands what the working arrangements or commitments are. To build your ships to be solid and unsinkable, consider revisiting some of the important relationships and partnerships in your life. Make sure you have mutual goals and expectations and that each other's needs are being met.

Execute with Care, Trust, and Integrity

A business partnership often contains an agreement, either verbal or written, where both parties are working together to execute, implement or accomplish something. Working together is one thing, but working together with care, trust, and integrity is the foundation and the key to a successful partnership. If you don't have a common endgame or shared vision, you may be operating in different directions, rather than working together toward a common outcome. This can be as simple as a working agreement with a client that outlines the expectations and terms, or a retirement plan for you and your spouse. But the key here is executing your agreement, which is getting things done together.

Exceed Others' Expectations

Sometimes in a partnership you might feel like *"I have given it all I've got!"* But both parties need to still always try and exceed what is expected so that no one gets complacent or taken for granted. Remember, the number-one reason customers leave is because they feel undervalued or ignored; it's not because of price. It's unlikely the customer is going to say, "You didn't pay attention to me," or "I really needed more from you." In business, remember the CPR strategy model and ensure you have retention strategies that are going above and beyond the customers' expectations.

How well are you exceeding the expectations in your personal relationships? I remarried eleven years ago and wanted to set expectations from the beginning. Does he expect me to have dinner on the table, the laundry done, and make sure the house is spotless? I sure hope not. But, we talked about this and other areas to be clear on what we could each expect. That way no one is disappointed. Now, it's fun to exceed expectations as part of our shipbuilding in the marriage. The small things can make the biggest difference. He loves it when I have dinner for him unexpectedly, or fold his shirts just the way he likes them.

Empathy and an Emotional Connection

Empathy is recognizing, perceiving, and directly feeling the emotion of another person. This is so important in both personal and professional relationships, yet doesn't come naturally for many. We recommend throughout *Race to Amazing* to work on strengthening empathy and begin to think with your head, heart, and gut. This will enable you to look at a situation in a different light, put yourself in the shoes of others, and begin to have more of an emotional connection with the other person.

Constantly Work on It

Business, like any successful marriage, takes constant attention and work. I see relationships fail often between managers and their employees because there is a lack of accountability or expectations aren't clear. In marriage, friendships, and family it can become constant work, yet easy to forget. If you're building, you're never leaving well enough alone.

When Grandma and I returned from our spa trip, Poppa was anxiously waiting for her in the kitchen; it had been the first time she had left him for a night. We walked in the door and she quickly went over to him and said, "Kiss me on the cheek, it smells like honey." He looked at her, then stared at me and in Poppa typical style said, "Well.. yunz don't look any different! I thought yuz were gett'n facelifts?" I think Poppa and Grandma could teach all of us a few things, as they were married for sixty-five years. I'm sure it was constant work for them, but humor helped. Poppa was a very special man, and I didn't want to have any regrets building my relationship with him, after my beloved grandmother passed away. At age ninety-two, I asked him to walk me down the aisle and give me away in my father's absence. It was a special day for both of us. It happened to be his "would be" seventieth wedding anniversary. He never had a daughter or wore a tux before. Without me asking, he would never have had the experience. And for me? Well, that day could not have been more perfect.

• •

Shipbuilding Activity

Take a moment and list the top three most important relationships and/or partnerships in your life.

1.

2.

3.

How can you use some of the concepts of shipbuilding to make your SHIPS better, stronger, and more meaningful?

What actions can you take to build the above SHIPS that matter most to your success and happiness?

CHAPTER 13—YOU ARE AMAZING

Like any great race, the finish line is the ultimate reward. Regardless of how long it took you to get there, or what place you were in, you made it. You finished. You achieved your goal and have to be feeling amazing.

Ultimately with *Race to Amazing*, I'm hoping that you discovered more about *you* and your strengths as a leader. How you can have a more effective management system and style. More importantly, how you can change to get better results through others with a "coaching approach" that serves, inspires, and teaches others. Leadership is influence, not a position. You got this!

Once you've reached the finish line, it's time to celebrate your victory. Reflect on the hard work—your preparation, dedication, and completion. Relish in that wonderful feeling of accomplishment.

Hopefully, you also experienced this as a personal race, to discovering not only who you are, but also who you want to *be*. *Be*coming takes continuous growth, so unfortunately your race may not actually ever end. I know that's not what you wanted to hear. You're amazing just the way you are. Let your *be*ing shine through by growing daily.

No Need to Do It Alone

We often hear "It's lonely at the top" from many of our successful sales leaders. There is no need to feel isolated when you reach an amazing sales leadership status. Don't forget: success isn't about how many hours a day you work, or even winning the race, but more about the positive impact you have had on others. You can't serve others without first serving and taking care of yourself. So make sure you make time to work on self-care and continued personal growth. Remember, when you're not growing, you're dying.

One way to stay on top of your game and ensure self-development is through participating in mastermind groups. Mastermind groups have emerged as a fresh new approach to personal and professional development and we are seeing an increasing number of executives and entrepreneurs getting involved in these types of programs.

At K.Coaching, our executive coaches are currently facilitating a number of mastermind groups. We also participate in mastermind programs to enrich our own professional development, and we can attest to the significant impact belonging to such a group can make on achieving goals and addressing challenges. We have seen first-hand how mastermind programs promote individual success, and we strongly encourage you to learn more about the concept and get involved at some level.

What Is a Mastermind Group?

In his book *Think and Grow Rich,* author Napoleon Hill defines "mastermind" as "the coordination of knowledge and effort of two or more people, who work toward a definite purpose, in the spirit of harmony." The mastermind is based on the concept that "no one does it alone." In other words, a small group or team working on the same issue will generate better results than a lone individual. Mastermind groups bring together like-minded individuals into an organized facilitated forum.

As a member, you brainstorm ideas and best practices that are critical to professional and personal success in a particular common area. A mastermind group is a great environment for receiving feedback, fielding challenges, and challenging others to implement new strategies to help personal and professional growth.

You can also join local or national organizations that have a mastermind or peer-to-peer forum component that brings together professionals from various industries with a common set of criteria and purpose. I've enjoyed, and received a lot of value from my experience as a forum member and on the board of directors for the local chapter of <u>EO – Entrepreneurs' Organization:</u> An international organization of successful entrepreneurs and startup businesses with mastermind-like forums as their foundation for presenting challenges and learning from other members' experiences.

How Do They Work?

Joining a mastermind program requires an investment of both time and money. Most groups are typically membership-based and necessitate a commitment to attendance and involvement. The forums are often professionally facilitated or moderated by a certified business coach or a group-assigned mentor.

A successful mastermind forum will establish ground rules, guidelines, or a forum constitution. There will be a member-created agenda with meaningful topics that build an environment of experience sharing, non-judgment, and confidentiality. In our experience, we found in-person masterminds more effective, but a committed and engaged group can still conduct valuable sessions via conference calls, Skype, or webinars.

What Can You Gain?

The dynamics of your group will highly influence the benefits that you receive, and will always be changing. It's important to understand the factors that make up these dynamics; as with any collective, it takes a bit of time for a group to develop into a safe, intimate environment. The beauty of most masterminds lies in their format: a confidential trusting coaching group, where you can share and learn about topics that are most important to you—business, personal, or family.

If you're interested in expanding your network and tapping into the experience, intelligence, and learning of other like-minded people, then joining a mastermind or peer group is a great start. Reach out to others in your industry, ask what other successful businesses are doing in this area, or give us a call at K.Coaching and let us point you in the right direction. For more information on our Race to Amazing Sales Leadership Masterminds, go to www.RaceToAmazing.com.

Remember, no one ever did it alone.

Word of the Year

Creating your vision and executing your strategy is a very big part of sales leadership success. But it's not always easy to stay focused, with the end in mind. Are you someone who creates New Year's resolutions at the beginning of the year only to find yourself in March already giving up? Or maybe you're a part of the 38 percent of people who don't set annual goals or resolutions in the first place. Regardless, if you're working on your personal Race to Amazing, it's likely that you have created some lofty goals and aspirations.

Studies show that the top four American resolutions are weight loss, improved finances, exercise, and getting another job. I typically create one personal and one professional resolution in January and try to stay on task with goals throughout the year. As I'm sure you can imagine, it's easier said than done. Excuses like "I don't have time" or "there are no parking spaces in the gym parking lot" are good ones for me.

Race to Amazing isn't a one-time resolution; it takes refreshing and continuous reminding to stay on track. Over the past few years I've started to create my Word of the Year, and I like to share this concept with our clients. What is the one word you could embrace throughout the year that would motivate and inspire you to reach your goals?

What I discovered were the reasons most resolutions don't work. They don't work well because they address only one level of your life: the *Do Level*. For example: "I'm going to get organized, lose weight, and spend more time with family." At the *Do Level* it can be overwhelming and difficult to stay on task, because there are so many to-do's to manage. When you create and commit to your Word of the Year, you focus on the BE level. What you want to BEcome as a result of all the doing. Examples from above might be: "I want to *be* more efficient, healthier, and a better mother." Or it might be "I want to *be* an amazing leader."

I know. It sounds a little woo-woo. I thought the same thing until I was introduced to this concept by my business coach, and then first worked through the exercise with a friend. My girlfriend and I were on a plane headed to Utah from the East Coast, with a lot of time to kill. So with a pen and cocktail in hand, we coached each other through the exercise and both landed on our perfect Word of the Year. Our words are very different, but they certainly embody who we are as individuals today, and what we aspire to *be*.

That first year my one word was jump, and it kept me focused on the actions that I needed to take that leap of faith into a new direction for the business, and land firmly on my feet. The following year, my word was unstoppable, which gave me the daily energy, confidence, and motivation to make the necessary changes, and not let anything or anyone get in my way.

Word of the Year Exercise

Go to www.RaceToAmazing.com and download the Word of the Year Exercise. The exercise is a worksheet that guides you through a series of thought-provoking questions. It starts out asking you to list the word or words that you're considering, and why you think they're the perfect words for you. Next, the exercise goes a bit deeper to ask "If you embodied this word daily, what would be different for you?"

It continues with a series of questions that gets you thinking about how your life would be different one year from now, if you were to live this word daily throughout the year. Then, begin thinking about what your year would look like if you ran in the opposite direction of your word.

Ultimately, you cross out and discard some original words and end up with the one word that you're certain to incorporate into your life. This makes goal-setting and the desire to create new proactive habits amazingly easy.

But don't take my word for it (no pun intended). I've done this exercise with many clients, friends, and family and they have all walked away with greater awareness, renewed energy, and a word they can live by.

The Finish Line

Just when you thought you were done, here are three tips to keep you growing in the right direction.

Own it. Look at where you're today, and how you got there. Take responsibility for the decisions you've made in your life and in your career. It's OK to look back in the rearview mirror, but don't spend too much time on shoulda, coulda, woulda. Don't let the past drain your energy. Owning it means accepting without excuses. Be proud of your accomplishments, your legacy, and the influence and positive impact you've had on others.

Go deeper. Keep searching for your true purpose, meaning, and passion. How can you lead your best life while serving others? Reflect often on your 10-year-old self, and your life experiences to understand your unique DNA, talents, and gifts. Who are you at your core, and how can you grow that seed daily?

Play big. Amazing sales leaders take calculated risks and they know how to execute. They know that Race to Amazing isn't about behavior modification, but heart transformation. Play big from your position of strength. Be *you*, not them.

We welcome you to join the community of Race to Amazing fans and friends for continued growth, inspiration, and motivation. Visit www.RacetoAmazing.com for more details and unlimited access to additional tools and resources to support you.

CHAPTER 14—WE'RE HERE TO HELP

"You had the power all along, my dear."

—Glinda the Good Witch, *The Wizard Of Oz*

Join the many Race to Amazing fans and sales leaders through our Race to Amazing (RTA) website and social media platforms, including our **Amazing Leaders** LinkedIn group. Become an RTA member, and take advantage of training coursework and mastermind groups.

Contact K.Coaching (https://www.kcoaching.com/) for more information on our **Race to Amazing Coaching Program**™. This program is an in-depth leadership coaching program for serious leaders and companies who are committed to personal and professional development. Our proven system is a fast track for implementing the changes you need to be an amazing, inspiring leader and get the results you want through others. This six-month coaching program can be conducted individually or with a team of sales leaders. It is designed to build awareness of your current leadership style and create positive changes toward improving personal and professional success.

Another option is the **RTA Sales Vault**™ – a membership site that gives you access to all of the RTA resources from the book and much more! You get 24/7, unlimited access to what you need when you need it, to support you on your path to becoming an amazing leader. The **RTA Sales Vault**™ includes a personalized **Learning Dashboard** with over thirty hours of online sales and leadership training through video learning, mobile-ready webinars, online testing, and certificates of completion. The **RTA Sales Vault**™ **Resource Center** contains blogs, articles, worksheets, and podcasts.

Go to www.racetoamazing.com for additional information on the above resources.

Finally, I hope that you enjoyed and benefitted from the experiences, exercises, strategies, and tactics in this book. If you did, I'd greatly appreciate you taking a moment to provide an honest review on www.amazon.com, where 85 percent of books are sold. Authors come to realize how important reviews are to the success of their books. I'm no exception. Even a short review is welcome. I thank you in advance and wish you the best in your Race to Amazing!

ACKNOWLEDGMENTS

I want to recognize the many family members, friends and colleagues who have supported me through this Race to Amazing adventure. First and foremost, to Kara and Karson, my two daughters, who sacrificed many years of not having their mom around. Thank you for understanding, being respectful, and loving me through the many difficult decisions I've made for our family. I am proud beyond words of the wonderful women you have become, for following your hearts and finding your passions in life.

To my mother who is always there for me, believes in me, and reminds me often that life is short and to slow down.

To my husband, best friend, and business partner Eddie, for all that you do for me and for us. For being the daily strength, providing the encouragement I need, and always supporting my crazy ideas.

This book would not even be possible without my former bosses, whether they were coaches, nice guys, or MIA. You have made me into the sales leader I am today. I learned something from all of you. I will always remember and forever appreciate Jay Sarver and Herb Gittelman for giving me my first sales position and opportunity. You discovered early on that I was motivated by a challenge and kept the fire burning.

To Harry Dochelli, the ultimate sales leader and professional. Under your leadership, I learned so much about myself and what I needed to do to be a better leader. I am thankful for you sending me to "Management Class," even though I thought I didn't need it, and the opportunity to learn the Professional Selling Skills curriculum and facilitate sales training for the company. It was that day, twenty-three years ago, that you said that I should consider a training and development career path. You always had a knack for identifying and bringing out hidden talents.

I will be forever grateful to Catherine Adams. In an industry with very few females, let alone female executives, you were a mentor and role model who opened doors, and ensured I had a seat at the table. Thank you for the many "stretch assignments" that gave me exposure to all aspects of business operations and sales enablement.

I want to acknowledge those individuals who believed in my vision when I founded K.Coaching. Inc. and supported me as a startup coaching, consulting, and training organization. To Mike Gentile, who gave me my first big break just months after starting my company, when he hired me for a training road trip covering ten cities in three months. This gave me tremendous exposure to my ideal market and potential clients. I am thankful for the opportunity and for the trust and confidence you had in me.

I want to thank Rick Toppin for providing me the opportunity to develop programs for your sales leaders, general managers, and customers. And Jim O'Brien and Bryan Wight for valuing learning and development, and the passion for seeing your customers succeed. And Sandra Williams for being by my side for the last eight years, and stepping up to take over as Chairman of the Board for OPWIL, our women in leadership nonprofit.

I realize that I would not be able to complete this book or implement our program without the hard work and dedication from the K.Coaching team. A special thanks to Eddie Moore, Susan Trumpler, Brittany DiCello, Meghan Munoz, Joyce Kinstle, and Bria Dixon. Your thought leadership, support, and loyalty mean the world to me. I could not have completed this labor of love without you.

A heartfelt thanks to Melissa G. Wilson and her team at Networlding for all of her coaching, expertise, and guidance throughout the writing and publishing process. I don't know anyone who has the level of passion that you do for your authors.

I'd like to give special recognition to my EO Forum group, "The Burning Moths," and to my mentor and friend, Brooks Bell for keeping me encouraged and motivated.

To all the guys and gals who have been listening, watching, coaching, and training with me over the past fifteen years. This book is for you, as a gift and a resource of the many models, lessons and coaching principles that you have embraced and use daily.

To all of our clients, and those I haven't met, I'm here to continue to inspire you to be your best and to help you get on the fast track to sales leadership success.

ABOUT THE AUTHOR

Krista S. Moore, president of K.Coaching, Inc., is highly recognized as an inspirational speaker and results-oriented executive coach. In 2003 she followed her entrepreneurial spirit and founded K.Coaching, Inc., after twenty years of sales leadership positions within the office products industry. Moore combines her real-life business experiences, certified business coaching, and motivational style to help others achieve outstanding success in their lives and careers.

In 2016, Moore and her team launched The Sales Vault™, an online business building learning management system utilized by thousands of sales professionals to enhance their sales strategies, training, and leadership development.

Moore is the host of *The Krista Moore Talk Show*. Her forthcoming book, *Your 10-Year-Old Self: The Powerful Process of Going Backwards to Move Forward In Your Life,* guides you through a process of exploring childhood memories in order to better understand your hidden talents, who you are at your core, and what is missing in your life.

Moore lives in Raleigh, North Carolina, with her husband and business partner, Eddie. Together they have three daughters: Kelsey, Kara, and Karson. She enjoys yoga, hiking, entertaining family and friends, playing golf, and igniting the potential in others!